# THE CURTAIN RISES

## VOLUME II

Also by Paula Gaj Sitarz:
*The Curtain Rises, Volume I:*
*A History of Theater from its Origins in Greece and Rome through the English Restoration*

# THE CURTAIN RISES

## VOLUME II

**PAULA GAJ SITARZ**

**BETTERWAY BOOKS**
Cincinnati, Ohio

97   96   95   94   93      5   4   3   2   1

Library of Congress Cataloging-in-Publication Data

Sitarz, Paula Gaj, 1955-
    A history of European theater from the eighteenth century to the present / Paula Gaj Sitarz. — 1st ed.
        p. cm. — (The Curtain rises ; v. 2)
    Includes bibliographical references and index.
    ISBN 1-55870-293-8 : $11.95
    1. Theater—History—Juvenile literature. I. Title. II. Series.
    PN2037.S53    1991 vol. 2
    792'.09—dc20                              92-39007
                                                  CIP
                                                   AC

*To Michael, Andrew, and Kate with love*
*and*

*To Helen Krich Chinoy*
*Who nurtured my love of theater history.*

# ACKNOWLEDGMENTS

Special thanks to the many individuals and institutions that were helpful and supportive:

To Claudia Mullaney and Michael Sitarz for their original illustrations.

To Joseph Medeiros for his invaluable photographic services.

To the staffs of the New Bedford Free Public Library, New Bedford, Massachusetts; Southworth Library, South Dartmouth, Massachusetts; North Dartmouth Library, North Dartmouth, Massachusetts; and the reference staff at University of Massachusetts (Dartmouth).

And to the following for help in gathering illustrative material:

Candi Adams, Public Relations Assistant, The Shakespeare Theatre at the Folger; Terry Ariano, Assistant Curator, Prints and Photographs Department, Museum of the City of New York; Dennis Behl, Press Director, The Guthrie Theater; Linda R. Betcher, Assistant to the Managing Director, Sacramento Theatre Company; Bibliothéque Nationale; Odile Blanchette, Maison de Victor Hugo; Elisabeth Brümmer, German Information Center; Peter Burrin, Head, Special Request Service, Central Office of Information; Mary Corliss, Assistant Curator, The Museum of Modern Art; Ruth Costelloe, Public Relations Assistant, Irish Tourist Board; Sylvaine des Fontenelles, Documentations, French Cultural Services; Dr. Gunter Duriegl, Director, Museen der Stadt Wien; Deborah Fehr, Williamstown Theatre Festival; Sarah R. Findley, Media Liaison, Alabama Shakespeare Festival; Sara Hope Franks, Press Director, Arena Stage; Janet Gersmiller, Office Manager, Michigan Information Transfer Service; Prindle Gorman-Oomens, Public Relations Director, Arizona Theatre Company; Cristofer Gross, Director of Public Relations, South Coast Repertory; Marion Hanscom, Head, Special Collections and Fine Arts Libraries, State University of New York at Binghamton; Jorund Lund Hansen, Administrative Secretary, The Norwegian Information Service; Dieter W. Kaisenberg, Educational Audio-Visual Director and Publisher, KaiDib Films; Lauri S. Lewis, Folger Shakespeare Library; Solvieg Linka, Swedish Information Service; Wendy C. Logan, Publicist, Asolo Center for the Performing Arts; Richard Mangan, Director, The Raymond Mander and Joe Mitchenson Theatre Collection; The Metropolitan Museum of Art; William A. Moffett, Librarian, The Huntington Library; Celia Morgan, Press Office, Royal National Theatre; Jeanne T. Newlin, Curator, Harvard Theatre Collection; Pioneer Theatre Company; Kent Politsch, Publicity Manager, Missouri Repertory Theatre; Sue Presnell, Reference Coordinator, The Lilly Library, Indiana University; Christopher Robinson, Keeper, University of Bristol Theatre Collection; Denise L. Rosen, Marketing Manager, Steppenwolf Theatre Company; James Seacat, Director, Public Relations and Marketing, Actors Theatre of Louisville; Chuck Still, Managing Director, Berkshire Theatre Festival; Bob Taylor, Acting Curator, The Billy Rose Theatre Collection at the Performing Arts Research Center of The New York Public Library; the TheatreMuseum, Munich; Tina Tryforos, Magnum Photos, Inc.; The National Theatre Society Limited, Abbey Theatre, Dublin, Ireland; Edwin Wallace, Victoria and Albert Picture Library; Zandra Wolfgram, Communications Associate, Great Lakes Theater Festival.

# CONTENTS

Note to Teachers and Librarians ..................................... 11

1. The Curtain Rises: On the Past ..................................... 13

2. Eighteenth Century England: The Age of Great Acting ................ 17

3. On the Continent: A Time for Ideas ................................ 29

4. The Nineteenth Century: Melodramas and Well-Made Plays ........ 41

5. Modern Theater Dawns: Realism and Independent Theaters ....... 57

6. Modern Theater Develops: Revolts Against Realism ................... 71

7. The Era of Isms: Theater Through the 1930s ................................ 79

8. Artaud and Brecht: Theater of Cruelty and Epic Theater ............. 93

9. Theater After World War II: Absurdists and Angry Young Men .... 101

10. European Theater Since 1960: Breaking Down Barriers ............... 111

11. With or Without a Curtain: European Theater Today .................... 129

Glossary ..................................................... 133
Suggested Reading ...................................... 139
Index ........................................................ 141

# NOTE TO TEACHERS AND LIBRARIANS

Often the history of European theater in the eighteenth and nineteenth centuries is glossed over because it was not a great period for dramatic literature. But what happened in the theater during this time does make fascinating reading for young people. Actors and actresses reigned supreme, and the stories of their lives paint a colorful picture. What youngster wouldn't be interested in reading about Henri-Louis Lekain, who became a great actor in spite of his bowlegs and flat, red, pimply face? What of Mademoiselle Dumesnil who ranted and raved on stage and died in a bed filled with chickens? The list of exciting and important performers is extensive and includes Sarah Bernhardt, who slept in a coffin, and George Frederick Cooke, whose body was buried without his head.

There are so many images from these centuries to entertain young readers: Colley Cibber appearing on stage with a wig so long and large it had to be carried; actresses wearing liquid white makeup that turned their faces into immovable masks; and William Charles Macready punching a man in the nose so he could use the flowing blood in his next scene.

Young readers exposed only to an encyclopedia article on European theater in the eighteenth and nineteenth centuries would miss out on so many interesting stories. They would not read about the many audience members who sat on the stage during performances or the riots that occurred in eighteenth century theaters. They would miss out on the colorful descriptions of nineteenth century melodramas in which a fire engine raced across the stage, an actress was tied to a railroad track, a dog was the star performer, or a huge tank was flooded to enact a sea battle. The nineteenth century was noted also for child actors, and most performers began acting as children, so there are many interesting tales about their early days in the theater, which often included hardships and struggles.

The modern theater began in the 1880s, and anyone who wants to appreciate theater today needs to look at the past century and all the innovations and experiments that took place. Particularly of interest to young readers are the many stories of courage, persistence, and obstacles overcome. So many theater artists who dared to present something new, such as Henrik Ibsen and George Bernard Shaw, were condemned, their works banned or censored. When John Millington Synge's work, *The Playboy of the Western World*, was first presented, seventy police surrounded the theater to prevent riots.

The Soviet director Vsevolod Meyerhold defended his artistic beliefs before a large gathering of Russian theater artists in the 1930s and was arrested, sent to a concentration camp, and later murdered. Fifty years later his fellow countryman, director Yuri Lyubimov, who at great risk presented plays that criticized the Soviet government, was made a nonperson in Russia and sent into exile.

Some theater artists succeeded in spite of dreadful childhoods. August Strindberg lived in a three-room apartment with ten people, and Sean O'Casey lived in the slums of Dublin and was illiterate until age fourteen. Maxim Gorky's life story is also an inspiration. Bullied by his grandfather and put out to work at age nine, he is now considered one of Russia's foremost playwrights.

There are many interesting images and tidbits from the theater of the twentieth century. Picture the eighteen-year-old André Antoine hauling his mother's furniture across Paris, France to a small rented space where he would direct new plays. Envision Alfred Jarry (whose play *King Ubu*, written when he was fifteen, would inspire theater artists everywhere) starting his meals with dessert and finishing with broth. Imagine the great Sir Laurence Olivier as a young actor fighting the giggles on stage and almost losing several acting jobs because of this problem. There are many moments too good to miss: experimental theater artists of the 1960s who smeared the audience members' laps with chocolate and eggs; Eugene Ionesco and other actors parading the streets with sandwich boards to get an audience for his play; and Joan Littlewood's performers improvising scenes on the roof of the theater.

The history of European theater from the eighteenth century to the present is fascinating. It is also like a series of mini-biographies of courageous and determined people. And it is a window on the political, social, and cultural situation of European countries during that time. Most of the plays discussed in this book are still staged today and read in schools. It is my hope that this book can make reading or seeing these dramas more enjoyable by putting them in their historical perspective, explaining how they were first produced, and sharing the background of the theater artists who created them.

# 1. THE CURTAIN RISES: ON THE PAST

Satin skirts, long and full, rustle backstage, and heels click on the wooden floorboards. The actors and actresses of an eighteenth century theater in Europe wait anxiously to appear. Before they walk on stage let's travel back in time to look at players of ages past, to see where and under what conditions they performed. Let's look at the theater traditions on which the eighteenth century performers were building.

## EARLIER THEATER TRADITIONS

The theater's roots lie at least 30,000 years ago when men acted out their hunts for food. Centuries later people sang and danced to honor their gods. These rituals were enacted the same way over and over again.

Plays, players, and playwrights appeared in the fifth century B.C., when Athens, Greece witnessed a golden age of fine drama. Tragedies told of gods, kings, and superhuman heroes, while comedies were humorous stories that centered on different character types. Comedies and tragedies were presented at an annual religious festival that all the people of Athens and surrounding lands attended for free. Three male performers, wearing masks, played the roles in each play in open-air theaters built in the hollow where hillsides met.

### Roman Theater

The state supported the Roman theater that followed. In Rome, plays were one of many entertainments offered to honor the gods and later presented just to amuse people. The theater was free to all, and people flocked to the massive, circular, open-air stone theaters. The plays were mainly comedies and pantomimes that relied on dance and song. Later, during the Roman Empire, the plays were full of violence and shocking scenes. Unlike the popular and

admired Greek actors, Roman actors and actresses were held in low regard. The new Catholic Church condemned them and their theater.

### Religious Drama

During the Middle Ages the Catholic Church used drama to educate people about religion. Short plays based on stories from the Bible were enacted in churches by priests and choirboys. Later, longer plays and series of plays about saints and people and events from the Bible were produced outdoors by amateur performers. Courtyards, market squares, and streets served as theaters. The action took place on several stages at once, on platforms where each scene was set in a structure called a *mansion*. This mansion looked like a small room with the front wall removed. Or the action took place on large wagons, each with its own mansion, which rolled through the streets. These religious plays could last for days and were offered only on special religious occasions. Entire communities watched the plays while seated on benches or standing in the street.

### Italian Renaissance

By the time of the Italian Renaissance the world had changed a great deal and so had the theater. Wealthy people mounted costly productions in small, private indoor theaters. The poorly written plays were of no consequence, only one of many entertainments that celebrated an important event like a wedding. On these social occasions the privileged audiences enjoyed the gorgeous costumes of the amateur performers, the beautiful painted settings, and the spectacular effects, including gods floating on a cloud.

### Commedia dell'Arte

A popular street theater called the *commedia dell'arte* also flourished during the Italian Renaissance. Professional actors and actresses who belonged to close-knit troupes acted on makeshift wooden platform stages for the crowds. These performers took the simple outline of a story, usually something comical, and improvised—made up—the words and actions. Each actor played the same character type—the lover, the mean father, the sneaky servant, for example—over and over again.

## Shakespearean England

Professional actors, but no actresses, performed in small, enclosed, roofless theaters during the Shakespearean era in London, England. The theaters attracted all types of people, who paid to see the plays offered on a regular, sometimes daily, basis. On a stage empty of scenery, with only a few props such as a rock or a chair, actors painted vivid pictures and told remarkable tales of heroes and kings. They breathed life into the brilliant plays of writers, including Christopher Marlowe and William Shakespeare, the latter considered the most outstanding playwright of all time.

## The Golden Age in Spain

Spain also enjoyed a "golden age" of playwriting during this period. Religious plays and secular plays, which included *cloak-and-sword* dramas, were enjoyed in open-air courtyard theaters or in the streets as the scenes of the play passed by on wagons. Professional actors and actresses performed the plays.

## Neoclassical Drama

Kings and members of the royal court controlled the fate of theaters during the French neoclassical period that followed. The theaters and performers existed to entertain the court and other members of the nobility. Authors had to pen their plays according to strict and specific rules. Known as neoclassical rules, they were loosely based on Greek drama. Permanent troupes of actors and actresses performed in indoor theaters converted from tennis courts.

Royal and wealthy audiences attended the indoor theaters of the English Restoration, for there, as in France, theater was a social activity for the privileged. The actors and actresses performed in tragedies similar to those in France and comedies that poked fun at the rich audiences who watched them.

## A VARIETY OF THEATER TRADITIONS

By the time the actors and actresses of the eighteenth century were ready to appear on stage, the European theater had witnessed many traditions. Theater had been part of a religious festival in fifth century Athens, Greece and during the Middle Ages. It had been supported by the state in ancient Rome. Royalty controlled theaters in Italy, France, and England during various ages, while theater was a professional business venture during the Shakespearean era.

Theaters had been located indoors and outdoors. There were permanent stages and temporary ones. Audiences viewed the play from a distance, far up a hillside, or from so close they could see the performers' eyes. The theater had appealed to small elite audiences, and it had attracted entire communities in a shared experience.

In different centuries a particular aspect of the theater—playwriting, acting, scenery—was more important than another. Drama was the most important element for the Greeks, the English of the Shakespearean era, and the French during the neoclassical period. There were few visual elements on stage, but the actors spoke the brilliant verse of outstanding playwrights. The formal, indoor theaters of the Italian Renaissance concentrated on spectacular visual effects, painted canvases that looked exactly like some Italian city, or stages flooded to enact sea battles, for example. In the *commedia dell'arte* the actors' skills were most important.

Performers sometimes included women; at other times men played all the roles. Players were amateurs—farmers, lawyers, aristocratic ladies—or professionals. Greek and Shakespearean actors were held in high regard; in other times and places actors were despised, refused Christian burial, and condemned by government officials.

## Children in the Early Theater

Children played their role in the early theater also. In the Middle Ages, boys and girls played the parts of angels in religious dramas. Some spun in giant globes suspended from the ceiling of a medieval cathedral. Child performers trained in *commedia dell'arte* troupes from the time they could walk. In the Shakespearean era young boys played most female roles. The English Restoration used children to introduce and end plays. Young boys in that era also served as pages to arrange the long trains of actresses' gowns when the actresses fell to the stage floor during death scenes. We will meet child performers again as we travel through the eighteenth, nineteenth, and twentieth century theaters of Europe.

As we journey forward, we will meet people who feel theater exists for a variety of reasons: to entertain, as a social occasion for a select group, as a ritual for few or many, to teach moral behavior, to make a statement, or to move the audience to change society or their own thinking. We will see how politics, science, technology, and world events affect the theater. We will see how theater is, has been, and will continue to be a reflection of the times in which it exists.

And now, we have kept the actors waiting long enough to come on stage and tell their story. Let's begin in eighteenth century England.

# 2. EIGHTEENTH CENTURY ENGLAND: THE AGE OF GREAT ACTING

Actresses with full, floor-length hoop skirts and powdered hair piled high atop their heads enter the stage through a door. The door is one of several at either side of the proscenium arch, the large "picture frame" that divides the stage area from the audience. The actresses walk onto the *apron*, or platform stage, that extends into the auditorium. Far behind them, in back of the proscenium arch, stands painted scenery. One actress steps forward to recite her lines and while she does the other actresses gaze at the audience.

In front of the actresses are the many gentlemen, ladies, and professionals crowded on backless benches in the pit, the U-shaped, slanted ground floor area of the auditorium. The jeweled, fashionable, and wealthy ladies and men fan themselves in

*The Theatre Royal Covent Garden in the eighteenth century. Reproduced by permission of The Huntington Library, San Marino, California.*

the boxes, partitioned areas that go around the pit from one side of the auditorium to the other. Tradesmen, businessmen, and their wives sit quietly in the gallery above, which also extends around the sides and back of the theater. In the upper gallery sailors and an assortment of less refined people jostle and settle themselves.

## THE EARLY EIGHTEENTH CENTURY

It is the beginning of the eighteenth century in England. The stage, auditorium, scenery, and costumes are not very different from those of the English Restoration that began in 1660 when King Charles II was restored to the throne after his exile in France. However, the audience is different and the world is changing.

During the Restoration, the theater was the plaything of the court. The aristocracy and the royals came to the theater to socialize and to watch witty, indecent comedies. Unlike King Charles II, Queen Anne, who began her reign in 1702, and her court were not interested in the theater but a growing middle class was.

The eighteenth century in England was a period of growing wealth. A middle class grew, consisting of tradesmen and professional people who wanted to attend the theater like the aristocracy. These new theatergoers were different from the select upper class audiences of the Restoration. The middle class did not appreciate wit, permissive behavior, or thoughtlessness in their lives or on the stage. They wanted drama with a moral or social lesson, and plays that let them sympathize with and pity the predicament of the characters. These merchants, industrialists, and their families wanted to see people like themselves — good and moral — on stage.

This was not a great century for English playwriting, however. Because more people attended the theater than in the past, the same plays ran for weeks, not a day or two. With less demand for new plays, playwriting became less profitable. Many authors were busy exploring other forms of writing, including essays and novels. These changes resulted in many mediocre dramas by inferior authors.

## The Licensing Act of 1737

The Licensing Act of 1737 was another reason for so few plays of lasting value being written during the eighteenth century. In 1737 Henry Fielding staged a play that made fun of the First Minister, Sir Robert Walpole, and it wasn't the first attack on the minister. In retaliation Walpole introduced a bill, which Parliament — the governing body — passed, giving the Lord Chamberlain the power to issue licenses to theaters. Drury Lane and Covent Garden in London were the only two theaters licensed.

The Lord Chamberlain, a member of the Queen's court, also was allowed to appoint an official to read and license plays. Many of the Lord Chamberlains were incompetent and used their powers as they saw fit. Since plays had to pass the approval of the censor, playwrights were discouraged from writing on many topics. They weren't allowed any controversial or negative comments on the Church or God, politicians or royalty. This censorship of drama in England continued until 1968.

## NEW STYLES IN PLAYWRITING

New tragedies were written according to the neoclassical rules the French had established, and the tragedies were not very successful. However, *The London Merchant; or, the History of George Barnwell*, written by George Lillo in 1731, was a turning point. The play is known as a *bourgeois* or domestic tragedy. In it a good young man's passion for an evil woman leads him to murder his old uncle for money. Eventually the young man is caught, repents, and is hanged.

Until this time tragedies had involved the lives of classical heroes, kings, and nobles. Lillo wrote about middle class characters, merchants, and apprentices. Instead of a tragic hero who is strong and important, Lillo's central character is weak, not powerful. Instead of the usual palaces and courts, the settings are counting houses and shops. Lillo showed that middle-class men, their problems and values, could be the subject of serious plays. Before, these characters had only appeared in comedies. Lillo's works

*Samuel Reddish as Young Beville in Richard Steele's play* The Conscious Lovers. *Courtesy Drama Library, Yale University.*

and ideas would have a great influence throughout Europe into the next century.

## CIBBER AND STEELE

Colley Cibber and Sir Richard Steele wrote many of the sentimental comedies that were popular for much of the 1700s. Cibber was a popular actor, manager, and teacher who wrote, among other plays, *Love's Last Shift; or, the Fool in Fashion*. Steele wrote his sentimental comedies, including *The Conscious Lovers*, to show people the proper way to behave, to show that being good is more desirable than being bad.

These sentimental comedies center on good, kind, well-meaning, middle-class characters who have social and family problems that are easily and happily solved. The plays include a moral lesson. The main character might be led into committing bad

deeds, but then realize before it's too late that he really wants to be a good person. Watching a sentimental comedy, the audience might see a character, perhaps a helpless mother or an innocent child, suffer through hard times, and then see her rescued from her sufferings and rewarded for being virtuous. In Cibber's *Love's Last Shift* a husband leaves his wife but is reunited with her at the end of the play, and everyone cries tears of joy.

Audiences sympathized with these characters and found them and their situations believable. Today the characters in these plays seem too good and their problems too easily overcome. The characters don't represent real people; the situations aren't resolved the way they would be in real life.

## GOLDSMITH AND SHERIDAN

It was not until the later years of the eighteenth century that Oliver Goldsmith and Richard Brinsley Sheridan wrote their brilliant and funny comedies. They wrote these plays in reaction to the sentimental comedies full of moral lessons. Goldsmith and Sheridan wrote witty plays with clever word play as the Restoration writers had, but without the indecency. Their comedies have complicated plots with

*A scene from a performance of* She Stoops to Conquer *by Oliver Goldsmith, directed by Joe Dowling and featuring Jane Pesci-Townsend, David Marks, and the Ensemble of the Arena Stage. Photograph by Joan Marcus. Courtesy Arena Stage.*

*A scene from David Garrick's production of* The School for Scandal *by Richard Sheridan, Drury Lane, 1777. Courtesy of The Billy Rose Theatre Collection, The New York Public Library for the Performing Arts, Astor, Lenox and Tilden Foundations.*

misunderstandings, disguises, mistaken identities, and surprise revelations. Often Goldsmith and Sheridan made fun of the way people in fashionable society behaved — their speech, manner, and attitudes.

Goldsmith wrote *She Stoops to Conquer*, which follows the humorous goings-on of the hero who thinks he is stopping at an inn, but who is really staying at his fiancée's home. The fiancée pretends to be a maid to encourage her love, who is too shy to win a lady. Sheridan's play *The Rivals* was produced when he was twenty-four. At the end of the first performance of Sheridan's *The School for Scandal* it is said the applause was so great that a passerby ran away because he thought the theater would collapse. In this play Sheridan makes fun of the activities and behavior of the fashionable people of the times. There is much scandal, gossip, and intrigue, and a young wife and old husband who quarrel with witty words.

As a youngster Goldsmith was ugly, small for his age, and pockmarked. At times he led an aimless and unhappy life. Sheridan was ignored by his teachers and teased by his classmates because his father was an actor. Sheridan hated the theater but turned to it for a short time as a way to make money when he was very poor. In spite of these early hardships both men wrote several fine plays which, with the excep-

tion of Shakespeare's, have been staged more than any English playwright's.

## RISE OF THE UNDERGROUND THEATERS

Drury Lane and Covent Garden, the two licensed theaters, were the only theaters allowed to present these dramas, tragedies, and sentimental and witty comedies. These plays were called "legitimate" drama, which meant that they were legal, licensed by the Lord Chamberlain. This term distinguished these plays from other forms of entertainment offered in minor, "underground," or illegitimate theaters, which also were allowed to exist.

In the nineteenth century the term "legitimate theater" became popular. It referred to comedies and tragedies as opposed to other entertainments like musical comedies and revues. The phrase "legitimate theater" is still used and it is often shortened to "legit." Today in the United States "legit" often refers to stage plays as opposed to movies and television shows.

Much of the population, especially workmen and their families, preferred to go to the underground theaters where they could enjoy puppet shows, concerts, ballad operas, and pantomimes. The ballad operas took popular plays, often about a current issue, and interspersed them with songs. The most famous ballad opera was *The Beggar's Opera* by John Gay, which made fun of the political situation and people's morals.

An almost illiterate man named John Rich made pantomime popular. Pantomime was a mixture of mime — silent acting — dance, and music. It included a comic story that featured the adventures of Harlequin, a funny and clever fellow who got himself into trouble and out again.

Managers of the underground theaters did find ways to get around the Licensing Act to present plays. One manager, Samuel Foote, invited people to a tea or chocolate party for which they paid, and then provided "free" entertainment — a play. Other managers charged for entrance to an exhibition of paintings or for a pint of beer, and then offered a "free" play.

## ACTORS OF THE DAY

In 1741, at an underground theater, Goodman's Fields Theatre, an amateur player who couldn't succeed at the licensed theaters appeared. His name was David Garrick. At the age of twenty-four he performed as Richard II in Shakespeare's play between two parts of a musical concert. Garrick was an immediate hit, the talk of the town. Each night the road to Goodman's Fields Theatre was blocked by the carriages full of people waiting to see Garrick act.

Garrick became one of the most influential and excellent performers of the age. Playwriting was at a low point, but the eighteenth century theater in England would come to be known as "The Age of Great Acting" because of Garrick and other fine actors and actresses. Plays were often written for specific performers, and these players often made dull plays successful.

Garrick showed audiences an acting style that was different from that of most performers of the time, perhaps with the exception of the Irish actor Charles Macklin, a former servant. The big-jawed Macklin became an overnight success when he treated the character of Shylock in Shakespeare's *The Merchant of Venice* seriously, with dignity, as a tragic person. Until then the role had been played comically. It seems like a small thing, but at the time it was sensational and caused an uproar. Actors weren't expected to be original. Traditionally, actors handed down their interpretation of characters, the way the lines should be read, and even how to move on stage. If a performer changed these interpretations, as Macklin did, it was considered radical.

### The Traditional Acting Style

Most players of the time, including Robert Wilks and James Quin, performed in a traditional way. The actor who was speaking would stand at the front of the stage and recite his lines to the audience. All lines were spoken in an artificial, heavy, exaggerated, and pompous or affected way. An actor would use drawn-out pauses or startling movements to create a dramatic effect. Performers didn't try to act the way they believed a character would in different situations or the way anyone did in real life.

When James Quin played the part of a great man in despair, he bellowed like a bull and beat his forehead. A large man with a strong voice, he appeared in this role wearing a green velvet coat embroidered down the seams, a huge wig that curled about his shoulders, and high-heeled, square-toed shoes. As Brutus in Shakespeare's *Julius Caesar*, Quin repeatedly thrust his left side into that of the actor playing Cassius. Each time, there was a shock as the hilts of their swords clashed. Quin posed, used formal gestures, and recited his lines in a mechanical sing-song.

Suzannah Cibber, who acted with Quin, also recited her lines in a sing-song for part of her career. One audience member reported that after Cibber recited two or three speeches he could tell what the

Mr. MACKLIN & Mrs. POPE *in the Characters of* SHYLOCK & PORTIA.

*Charles Macklin as Shylock in* The Merchant of Venice *by William Shakespeare. From the art collection of The Folger Shakespeare Library.*

rest of her performance would be like. She never varied her voice whether she was saying something sorrowful or just relaying a message. This was the accepted acting style of the time.

## David Garrick

Enter David Garrick, former wine merchant, playwright, poet, producer, manager, actor, who broke the rules and acted in a more natural style than most performers. He studied people, watched how they actually behaved, and used these observations in his acting. When Garrick developed the part of King Lear in Shakespeare's play he studied the behavior of an acquaintance who had gone insane after accidentally killing his young daughter. Lear, who goes mad at the end of the play, was one of Garrick's greatest roles.

Even though he was only about five feet, five inches tall and not very handsome, Garrick would walk on stage and immediately capture the audience's attention by speaking naturally and varying his tone of voice depending on the emotion he was supposed to show. He also used a variety of gestures and movements to express his character's feelings. He did unusual things like shrugging and putting his hands in his pockets rather than standing stiffly. Many people talked about Garrick's "eye," his expressive dark eyes, which they said suggested emotions. When Garrick played the comic role of Abel Drugger he moved his eyes, lips, knees, and head in

*David Garrick in the title role of* Richard III *by William Shakespeare. Courtesy Drama Library, Yale University.*

certain ways to say something about the character. Instead of acting each role in the same way, he tried to make each character an individual. Garrick was versatile and played a wide range of parts especially in Shakespeare's plays. Garrick is considered by many the first superstar of the English stage, while others call him the greatest actor of the English theater. Garrick developed a new style of acting but he did much more. At the age of thirty he became the manager of The Theatre Royal, Drury Lane, and there he made many reforms in the theater. Garrick was an actor-manager. He staged and starred in most of the theater company's productions. Many English actor-managers would follow in the decades ahead.

## Garrick as Actor-Manager

Garrick brought the best performers to Drury Lane, including the comedienne Kitty Clive. She began her career playing small parts at Drury Lane and went on to play leading roles opposite Garrick for twenty-two years. When the beautiful and witty Peg Woffington walked on stage dressed as a gentleman, the audience went wild. They loved to see her in a "breeches part," a role in which she played the part of a man. Woffington retired from acting when her tongue became paralyzed while she was on stage.

Garrick tried to make his performers more unified in their acting style. Before Garrick, players acted as they wished, showing off their individual talents without regard for their fellow actors. Garrick expected his performers to attend rehearsals on time, to know their lines, and to learn his style of acting.

Garrick's Drury Lane operated on a *repertory* system, staging different plays every night. Each performer in the company was assigned a large number of roles and was expected to perform any one of them on twenty-four hours' notice. Once a performer was given a part it was his to play for as long as he was a member of the company. David Garrick had ninety-six roles.

## Garrick's Influence on the Theater

Garrick made another important reform in the theater, but it wasn't easy to do. Since Shakespearean times spectators had been allowed to sit on stage during the performance. In the eighteenth century the situation became intolerable. Sometimes the spectators on stage, sitting on rows of raised seats, blocked the scenery or made it hard for a performer

*Spectators on stage during a performance of John Gay's* The Beggar's Opera. *Courtesy Drama Library, Yale University.*

to move without touching someone in the audience. Peg Woffington once played the role of Cordelia in *King Lear* with a spectator's hand around her waist. When Suzannah Cibber played Juliet in Shakespeare's *Romeo and Juliet*, over one hundred spectators, some crying, sat in the tomb area with her as she played her death scene.

Performers often had to fight their way through the spectators to get on stage. In one performance of *Hamlet* the actor playing the title role was supposed to have his hat fly off his head and then complain of the cold. When he played the scene, however, a woman in a red coat crossed the stage, picked up the hat, and placed it back on the actor's head. The audience laughed.

David Garrick didn't think these disruptions were funny. In 1762 Garrick remodeled the inside of Drury Lane to fit more seats in the auditorium, and he banished spectators from the stage. He also banned gentlemen from wandering backstage to watch the play. On occasion the audience saw a man's brocaded coat and powdered wig poking out from the scenery. Garrick also forbade men from going into the *green room* to flirt with the actresses. The green room was a furnished area, decorated in green, where men could meet the performers in between their appearances on stage. Audience members during the eighteenth century were fascinated with actors and actresses, especially with their private lives.

Audiences didn't become well-behaved because of Garrick's reforms. Before the curtain rose they often shouted, yelled, and jeered. The motley crowd in the upper gallery sometimes roared like lions, hooted like owls, and mewed like cats. Audiences wielded a lot of power, too. If they didn't like an actor or a play, they came to the theater night after night to boo and hiss. Their actions could stop a play from being staged again.

*A riot at Covent Garden Theatre in 1763. Reproduced by permission of The Huntington Library, San Marino, California.*

## Rioting and Rowdy Audiences

Riots in the theater occurred on several occasions. Audiences rioted when they felt their rights were being abused or as a stronger protest against a performer or a new play. Sometimes spectators tried to storm the stage, smash scenery, and stop the performance. This happened to Garrick when he tried to make audiences pay full price even if they came toward the end of the performance. A gang was organized, who smashed woodwork and shattered lights.

In 1721 during a performance of *Macbeth* at Lincoln's Inn Fields a spectator crossed the stage to talk to a friend behind the scenes. The theater manager yelled at the spectator, who then slapped the manager across the face. When the manager slapped him back, people drew their swords. The spectator was forced to leave, but he returned with other men who wrecked furniture and equipment in the theater. The military ended the riot and the offenders were taken to court. After this, two armed guards with muskets stood at both sides of stages during performances.

In 1755 benches were torn up and scenery destroyed at the Drury Lane Theatre. In 1776 a man was thrown from the gallery. He saved himself by hanging from a chandelier. If you look at pictures of some theaters of the time, you will see spiked railings along the front of the stages. The railings were to keep spectators from invading the stage.

Even when audiences weren't rioting they might call each other names. Sailors and footmen in the hot and cramped upper gallery might pelt the professional people seated in the pit with rotten apples, walnut shells, orange peels, or water. In 1755 a hard piece of cheese hurled from the upper gallery hurt a young girl in the pit. One night a man threw a keg full of liquor. As a young man James Boswell once entertained the crowd at the Theatre Royal, Covent Garden by mooing like a cow during a performance.

If the play didn't begin on time some spectators rapped their sticks and canes on the floor. Audiences also demanded their money's worth, so a long program was necessary. Usually an evening's performance, which began at six p.m., consisted of a tragedy, a comic skit, a ballet or pantomime, dancing, and music. The entertainment lasted three to five hours.

Conditions weren't easy for the players. They had to work hard to grab everyone's attention. Maybe that's another reason such excellent actors and actresses developed during the 1700s in England.

## STAGING CHANGES

David Garrick reformed actors and spectators but he did not stop there. When Garrick enlarged the auditorium to add more seats and accommodate larger audiences, this caused changes in the stage and it meant changes for the performers. The apron stage, where the performers recited their lines, had projected into the auditorium. Now it was cut by half. Because of this the proscenium arch was narrowed. Instead of the arch being deep enough to have two or three doors on each side, new stages had one door on each side of the proscenium.

Because the apron stage and the proscenium arch were shortened, actors entered the stage more often through the scenery on either side of the stage, instead of through the doors. Performers also recited their lines in back of the proscenium picture frame, not in front of it. This put the actors closer to the scenery and farther away from the audience. This trend and the move toward larger theaters with deeper, wider stages continued for many years.

### Lighting

In 1763 Garrick went on a tour of theaters in Italy and France, and he returned with ideas to change the stage. He also had ideas about lighting, which he instituted at Drury Lane. Lighting had been a problem in indoor theaters. Until Garrick's time the theaters were lit by large hoop-shaped chandeliers with rings of candles. The chandeliers were lowered before the play began and two servants with candle lighters lit the chandeliers, which then were raised to their positions above the audience and the actors. The hoops blocked the view of audience members in the galleries and offered poor lighting in back of the proscenium.

Garrick moved the chandeliers from the front to behind the proscenium, out of sight of the audience.

The audience also didn't see the candles standing in holders behind the scenery, one above the other in wooden frames. Now the whole audience had a clear view of the stage. The back of the stage and the scenery were better lit, not dim and hard to see as before. The performers who began to perform in this space more often could also be seen better.

Border lights—a row of lights along the front of the proscenium floor—provided illumination, too. All lights had tin reflectors attached to them, which could increase the intensity of the light. The reflectors could be directed toward or away from the stage. Now there was better control of the brightness of the light and its direction.

## Scenery

Under Garrick's guidance more changes followed. Garrick had new ideas about scenery. For the first three-quarters of the eighteenth century new scenery was unusual. The same *sets*, depicting palaces, gardens, temples, and prisons, for example, were used in play after play. A set was made up of several parts. There were three pairs of "side-wings." These were created by painting a scene on *flats*— canvas stretched on wooden frames. The flats were arranged one behind the other, parallel to the stage front on either side of the stage. The set also had a *backdrop*—a scene painted on canvas and hung at the back of the stage. Or the set had *shutters*—two painted flats moved together at the back of the stage. Painted pieces of scenery called *borders* were hung from the top of the stage to complete the set. The flats stood in grooves, narrow channels attached to the floor, and could be shoved on or pulled back along the grooves by scene shifters who moved the scenery at the sound of a whistle.

Garrick thought that specific settings should be designed for certain plays instead of using general settings over and over for all plays. In 1771 Garrick brought Philippe Jacques de Loutherbourg, a great scenic artist from Europe, to Drury Lane to carry out some of his ideas.

De Loutherbourg brought more realism into the painted stage sets. He painted scenery that represented real places, like Derbyshire in England. He also used a variety of sets for one play. In 1772 *The Grecian Daughter* had more than eight sets, including a cavern, a temple, a fortress, and a prison cell. The scenery wasn't placed parallel to the stage either, but at irregular intervals. The backdrops had pieces cut from them to reveal scenes off in the distance. De Loutherbourg also used silk screens and gauze curtains of different colors placed before lights to suggest moonlight, fires, volcanos, rain, and rising and setting suns. David Garrick was pleased with de Loutherbourg's innovations.

Garrick was a genius — actor, director, manager, and playwright—who made many changes in the theater. Garrick also raised the social status of performers. He even started an Actor's Fund to help actors when they retired. He was friendly with many noblemen of the day, and his theater, Drury Lane, became one of the most respected institutions in London. When Garrick died, his funeral was held at Westminster Abbey in London, where kings, queens, and other notables are buried.

Garrick came a long way from his first efforts as an actor. In those early years he feared that his friends would shun him. He hadn't told his family about his acting because acting and theaters didn't have a good reputation at the time. Later, Garrick wrote a letter asking his brother not to be ashamed of him for becoming an actor.

## OTHER GREAT ACTORS

It's easy to think of the theater in eighteenth century England as the theater of David Garrick. There were, however, many great players during "The Age of Great Acting," some of whom we have met already. The playwright Colley Cibber also acted, against his family's wishes. Cibber didn't have a great voice or physical appearance, but he studied hard and became an excellent comedian. Hannah Pritchard was one of the great tragic actresses of the century who adopted Garrick's style of acting. John Philip Kemble was a star during the last decades of the eighteenth century, and his sister Sarah Kemble Siddons was an actress who was considered Garrick's equal.

## Sarah Siddons

Sarah Siddons was the eldest of twelve children. She traveled and appeared on stage throughout her childhood with her father's company in the provinces. At eighteen Sarah Kemble married William Siddons. By the age of twenty when Sarah appeared at Drury Lane she was a mother. Sarah Siddons failed as an actress in the London theater. She returned to the theaters in the provinces, gained more confidence, and became a better actress.

Several years passed. A man from Drury Lane saw Siddons perform and asked her to return. "What to do?" Sarah wondered. Should she return to London and possibly fail again? By now Sarah had three children and she decided to try again for their sake. This time she was a hit in London.

Sarah Siddons became the leading tragic actress of the eighteenth century. Described as a beautiful, intelligent, dignified woman with a rich, expressive voice, Siddons was leading lady at Drury Lane for twenty-seven years. Sarah Siddons became emotionally involved in each part she played and, after some performances, Siddons cried from the emotion of the role until she returned home at night.

Sarah Siddons also made innovations in women's costumes. Most actresses wore the fashionable clothing of the time, as expensive as they could afford. Some actresses had their own seamstresses to sew costumes for them or had their gowns made in Paris. Sometimes their outfits were trimmed with gold and silver. For one of her costumes, the actress Mrs. Bellamy added diamonds to a gown once worn by a real princess. It was a free-for-all, with performers deciding what they would wear, and there were some odd sights on stage. If a poor actress played a queen, she looked shabby next to a servant in satin shoes played by a wealthy actress.

Tragic actresses who played roles like Cleopatra or Queen Elizabeth wore decorated long, wide hoop skirts and displayed powdered hair piled high atop their heads. Even actors wore high wigs. It is said that Colley Cibber once came on stage followed by a wig so large that it had to be carried.

In tragedies Sarah Siddons wore her hair smooth and braided. She wore a simple robe draped about

*Sarah Siddons as "The Tragic Muse." Reproduced by permission of The Huntington Library, San Marino, California.*

her like a Greek goddess. It wasn't historically accurate, but it was a step in that direction.

## IMAGINE ATTENDING A PERFORMANCE

The actors and actresses in their variety of costumes once again wait in the wings to appear on stage. You will be attending the performance, but first you have to get to the theater and your seat. You descend from your carriage and walk along an alley-way, past inns and houses to a small doorway. The ticket-seller hands you your printed ticket from her small cubicle.

You walk along a dark tunnel and then wait for the doors of the pit to open, while trying to avoid the pickpockets. When the doors open, there's a wild rush as everyone tries to get in first. The seats aren't reserved so people push and scream and clamber over benches to get the best seats. You struggle in your long, wide skirt and your friend loses his hat.

Somehow you find a good seat and wait for the curtain to rise.

This theater and many others are full on most evenings in eighteenth century England. Theaters on the Continent of Europe are busy too. Italian scenic designers are creating dazzling, massive sets, France is enjoying its own age of great acting, and in Germany theater is finally coming to life.

# 3. ON THE CONTINENT:
# A TIME FOR IDEAS

If you could travel to the major theaters on the continent of Europe during the eighteenth century, you would see the old battling with the new. In Italy one playwright hates the work of a second writer, while in France two actresses argue for their individual styles of acting on the same stage. Performers and playwrights in Germany also disagree on what plays should be written about and how they should be acted.

Much of what you see during your journey is similar to the eighteenth century theater in England, although the people and places are different. Playwriting isn't outstanding but the acting is memorable. Many of the problems are the same as in England, too, like getting rid of the spectators on stage. By the end of the century when you visit the state-supported theaters in western Europe you see that they have much in common. The playhouses are large and ornately decorated. The theaters have horseshoe-shaped auditoriums, and the seating is divided into pit, boxes, and galleries. You see the proscenium arches and the settings that combine painted scenes on wings, shutters, and borders. These features were developed by the Italians during the Renaissance of the fifteenth century.

## ITALIANS SET THE STAGE

The Italians continued to create spectacular painted scenery for the stage in the eighteenth century. The most influential designers of stage settings were members of the Galli-Bibiena family. They painted settings with such fancy columns, high curved arches, and enormous stairways that the audience felt they were looking at some vast space. Actors looked like ants in front of a castle hallway with a high, vaulted ceiling. Streets painted on canvas appeared to go on forever.

The Galli-Bibienas designed most of their settings for the opera, which was the favorite entertainment in Italy. Opera is a sung form of storytelling with elaborate costumes and settings. The Italians

*A design for an opera by Giuseppe Galli da Bibiena. By permission of The Metropolitan Museum of Art, The Elisha Whittelsey Collection, The Elisha Whittelsey Fund, 1951 (51.501.2731).*

enjoyed private entertainments, street festivals, and spectacles, too. They also witnessed a battle fought in Italian drama between Carlo Goldoni, a writer and lawyer, and Carlo Gozzi, a former aristocrat, which you will hear more about shortly.

The *commedia dell'arte* was a fun type of street theater developed during the Italian Renaissance. Audiences laughed at the different character types, like the lovers, the bragging soldier, and the tricky servant, who hurtled through one complicated incident after another. The professional *commedia* players improvised many of their lines and actions, and used *lazzi*, practical jokes, to entertain the crowds. The *commedia dell'arte* was still popular during the eighteenth century, but it was worn and repeating itself.

## THE BATTLE OF GOLDONI AND GOZZI

Carlo Goldoni decided to change the commedia. He turned the skeleton plot outlines into written comedies with no room for the actors to improvise. He tried to get rid of the masks that were the trademark of the commedia performers. Goldoni changed the character types into more realistic roles. He used his plays to comment on the world around him and how he felt people should behave. Goldoni made the *commedia* more like traditional comedy. Several of Goldoni's plays are still staged today.

Carlo Gozzi loved all the things about the *commedia* that Goldoni wanted to destroy, and he hated Goldoni for his reforms. He said that Goldoni sapped the life and fun out of the *commedia*. Gozzi kept the character types with their masks, and he allowed the actors to improvise lines and action. He changed the subjects of the plays, however. Gozzi wrote fairy tales about magicians, fabulous animals, wizards, and mind-boggling apparitions. So, for example, *commedia* characters found themselves transported to the castle of phantom kings where they took part in impossible, bizarre adventures.

The *commedia* had one last moment of glory, but by the end of the eighteenth century it was gone. The Italians flocked to opera houses, and comedies and tragedies were ignored for over one hundred years.

## PARIS—THE THEATRICAL CENTER OF EUROPE

Paris, France, not Italy, was the theatrical center of Europe during the eighteenth century, and other countries still judged their drama against the French. There wasn't much new to judge against, though. The only notable writer of tragedy in France during this time was Voltaire (Francois-Marie Arouet), playwright, philosopher, and friend of performers.

### Voltaire

Voltaire declared that the neoclassical rules, developed by the French during the seventeenth century, were like a straitjacket on writing. These rules stated that tragedies had to be written about legendary heroes, gods, and kings. According to these rules, tragedies had to have only one main action or story that took place in one location in a twenty-four hour period. Voltaire tried to write against the rules by introducing subjects from French mythology and history. He also introduced ghosts and some scenes of violence on stage, which had been forbidden. Voltaire's reforms were limited and most French tragedies written during the eighteenth century were dull.

### Denis Diderot

Denis Diderot developed *le drame bourgeois*—bourgeois drama about middle-class everyday life—similar to George Lillo's dramas in England. Diderot wanted to show how his characters are controlled by the society in which they live. French playwrights, including Pierre-Claude Nivelle de la Chaussée developed *comédie larmoyante* or "tearful comedy"—plays similar to the sentimental comedies in England. In these plays the cultured, educated, middle-class hero and heroine suffer misfortunes and are persecuted, but all ends happily for them. The message of these plays is that it is better to be good than to be bad.

### Pierre de Marivaux

Pierre de Marivaux enjoyed writing plays about characters falling in love. Sometimes two characters, usually a master and a servant, exchange costumes

*A scene from a production of* Les Jeux de l'Amour et du Hasard *by Pierre de Marivaux. Courtesy of The French Cultural Services.*

to impersonate each other so they can test their lovers' faithfulness. What made Marivaux's plays different from other comedies is that he wrote about the feelings and inner struggles of the characters, not just their actions. Marivaux's plays weren't appreciated until the twentieth century.

## Pierre de Beaumarchais

It wasn't until the late eighteenth century that France had an outstanding writer of comedies, Pierre Augustin Caron de Beaumarchais. Beaumarchais was a free spirit who led an interesting and sometimes dangerous life. He tutored King Louis XV's daughters on the harpsichord and spent ten years as a secret agent. Beaumarchais smuggled weapons and ammunition to the colonists during the American Revolution, and during the French Revolution he tried to help the revolutionaries against the aristocrats. Beaumarchais's family was imprisoned, his money was taken, and Beaumarchais barely escaped being beheaded.

Beaumarchais wrote witty satires that poked fun at and criticized the French aristocrats who controlled the government and other institutions. His most notable plays are *The Barber of Seville* and *The Marriage of Figaro*, which later became famous operas. These plays reflect how much anger and hate the common people felt toward the wealthy aristocrats in France who still controlled society. *The Marriage of Figaro* was banned by King Louis XVI for five years, and when *Figaro* was finally performed it caused a riot.

The main character in this play, Figaro the barber, stood for all the French people who felt they were used by the upper class. The play is a comedy with lots of laughs, but underneath audiences sensed Figaro's desire for freedom and equality. These were dangerous ideas to the rulers. Fiction became reality in 1789 when the common people in France rebelled against the King, overthrew the government, and beheaded many aristocrats during the French Revolution.

## Theater Before the Revolution

Until the French Revolution, the heart of French theater was the Comédie Française in Paris—the "Theater of the King's Great Actors." France, like England, enjoyed an age of great acting during the eighteenth century. Most of the talented performers were members of the permanent company of actors at the Comédie Française, which remained the only government-approved playhouse for comedies and tragedies in France. Since there were no great plays, many existing plays were translated and adapted. Sentimental comedies and bourgeois dramas were staged at unlicensed "booth theaters" on the Boule-

*Sarah Bernhardt as Adrienne Lecouvreur. Courtesy of The Billy Rose Theatre Collection, The New York Public Library for the Performing Arts, Astor, Lenox and Tilden Foundations.*

vard du Temple in Paris.

At the beginning of the century most actors were very formal, careful to pronounce their lines clearly and act dignified, or they recited their lines in an exaggerated way like James Quin of England. Performers didn't try to give meaning to what they said; they just wanted to show off. The biggest question an audience had was, "How will so-and-so recite her lines?" Throughout the century, however, individual talented players attempted a more natural style of acting just as David Garrick did in England.

## Actors and Actresses

Adrienne Lecouvreur was raised and educated under miserable conditions. When she was thirteen she joined an amateur troupe of performers and later became a popular actress at the Comédie Française. Adrienne Lecouvreur was slender with a delicate face and large expressive eyes. She was an intelligent actress who said "no" to chanting her lines and introduced more natural speech. People said that when she acted "her heart spoke."

Michel Baron returned to the stage at the age of sixty-seven after a thirty-year retirement to play opposite Lecouvreur. Baron was orphaned at an early age. He became a member of an acting company called the "Little Actors of the Dauphin" and later was the star of the troupe. Eventually he became the greatest actor of the French stage. He neither delivered his lines in a sing-song nor in a ranting way.

Baron listened to the other actors and reacted with his body and his face to what was said. Most actors didn't do this. They stood without expression until it was their turn to speak. Baron also talked as if he were having a real conversation, also unusual. As a young actor Baron shocked audiences by letting his hands go above his head. This gesture was against the rules of acting.

French theatergoers watched a rivalry between two actresses and two different acting styles at the Comédie Française. The actresses, who starred in tragedies, were Claire-Josèphe-Hippolyte Leris de la Tude Clairon—Mademoiselle Clairon—and Marie-Francoise Dumesnil—Mademoiselle Dumesnil. Mademoiselle Clairon studied each part carefully and

TALMA,

*Rôle de Néron dans Britannicus.*

*Publié par Blaisot.*    *Galerie Universelle.*

*François-Joseph Talma as Nero in* Britannicus. *Courtesy Drama Library, Yale University.*

*Jean Antoine Watteau's painting* The French Comedians, *showing the elaborate costumes of French actors and actresses in the eighteenth century. The Metropolitan Museum of Art, The Jules Bache Collection, 1949 (49.7.54).*

*Henri-Louis Lekain and François Vestris in a scene from* Semiramis *by Voltaire. Courtesy Drama Library, Yale University.*

planned how she would move, gesture, and speak. On stage Clairon portrayed her character by repeating what she had practiced, but she never felt any emotion from what she portrayed.

Mademoiselle Dumesnil left her acting to inspiration, the spur of the moment. Often, she entered the stage without knowing what she was going to say. Dumesnil would recite many of her lines carelessly, especially in the quiet, restrained, calm scenes. In scenes where she had to show great feeling, Dumesnil cried, used exaggerated gestures, and displayed much emotion. Once she made an audience cry for an entire play. Often Dumesnil went through so many quiet and then loud, raging moments that people accused her of being drunk on stage. Dumesnil died in an equally dramatic way, in a bed filled with chickens.

The other outstanding male performers in addition to Michel Baron were Henri-Louis Lekain and François-Joseph Talma. Lekain became a skilled actor in spite of his bowlegs, hollow cheeks, small snub nose, flat, red, pimply face, and harsh voice. Lekain and Talma agreed that actors should use their voices, gestures, movement, and costumes to create a character. They felt actors should move around more instead of stiffly reciting long speeches. Also, they said that lines should be spoken, not howled. Audiences were shocked by the idea that acting should be more like real life. To them, acting was something apart, something different and more perfect than real life. In 1756 when Lekain appeared in a role with messy hair, bare arms, and bloody hands, audiences were outraged.

## Costumes and Makeup

Lekain and Talma tried to get actors to wear costumes that reflected the period in which a play was set. Actors usually wore the same costume for all parts. If you watched an eighteenth century French actor, he would be wearing a large wig and a three-cornered hat with large bunches of feathers. Under his gilt chest armor was a silk shirt with wide sleeves and lace cuffs. Below the armor was a small, round wicker frame called a *tonnelet*, which had a short skirt attached to it that fell to the actor's knees. The costume was completed by a wide sword belt with a small dagger, fringed gloves, silk stockings, and low embroidered boots with high red heels. Lekain and Talma convinced a few actors to get rid of their fringed gloves, huge wigs, and feathered hats, but it wasn't easy. Part of being a performer was "dressing up."

Mademoiselle Clairon tried to make changes in women's costumes. She convinced actresses to stop using liquid white makeup, which turned their faces into immovable masks. It was more difficult to get actresses to change their fashionable costumes because women enjoyed their huge wigs decorated with diamonds and feathers. They liked appearing in their long, bouncing court dresses with fringe, lace, and bright ribbons. When Clairon appeared on stage in a simple, flowing robe she was called "courageous."

In plays set in exotic Eastern countries, actors and actresses might suggest the location by adding some accessories like jewelry, ribbon, or a headpiece to their usual costumes. But it would be some time before costumes accurately represented a specific place and time.

By the end of the century, even though there were many excellent performers, actors were still considered rogues and vagabonds and were excommunicated from the Church. When Adrienne Lecouvreur died, her body was wrapped like a package, placed on a cart, and driven at midnight to a marshy area. With no funeral service, Adrienne Lecouvreur was laid in the ground, no gravestone to mark the spot. It wasn't until 1789 that the National Assembly in France gave citizenship to "Jews, Protestants, and actors."

## THEATER IN GERMANY

While theaters were established in England, Italy, France, and Spain, Germany was an unsettled region, often at war. It consisted of over three hundred states, dukedoms, duchies, and principalities, but had no main city like Paris or London where a theatrical center could develop. The courts had their visiting French actors, opera, and ballet, but the public had no permanent theaters. Townspeople enjoyed the improvisations and farces, comedies with vulgar dialogue, wild action, and exaggerated characters, which traveling troupes performed on flimsy platform stages. The unsophisticated audiences especially liked plays about the famous German clown Hanswurst (Jack Sausage), with his acrobatic tricks and fooling.

The companies of German players were poor, uneducated, and not well trained. If they were lucky, they were invited to stay in a town or at a duke's court for several weeks or months. Often, however, they piled into wagons, traveled from town to town in rain, snow, and wind, and ate only when they had enough money. The wealthy and members of the Church called this sorry theater "worthless." Clergymen denounced the players as "sinful liars."

### Johann Gottsched and Carolina Neuber

This sad state of public theater in Germany reached a turning point in 1727. Johann Christoph Gottsched, a playwright, and Carolina Neuber, a leading actress

*Carolina Neuber. By permission of Deutsches TheaterMuseum, Munich.*

who had formed a professional acting company, agreed to work together to reform the theater. Gottsched tried to stage French tragedies. Neuber demanded that players memorize their lines and attend long, careful rehearsals. Neuber tried to raise the status of performers by insisting that they live good, moral lives. She watched their private lives and had the unmarried actresses room with her and help with chores.

Audiences squirmed through the classical plays offered, and they shouted for Hanswurst. When Neuber clothed performers in Greek costumes, not contemporary clothes, the audience thought it was a joke. In Hamburg, Germany, Carolina Neuber yelled at the audience for not appreciating her reforms. Gottsched and Neuber didn't really fail, though. They were pioneers who paved the way for other troupes. The modern German theater began with them.

### New Playwriting Trends

In the mid-1700s Gotthold Ephraim Lessing became

Germany's first important dramatist. He argued with Gottsched that the French tragedies were too stiff and formal for audiences. Lessing told playwrights to use ancient Greek drama and English drama as their models. "Read Shakespeare and use his free-flowing and imaginative style," Lessing suggested.

Lessing's play *Miss Sara Sampson* became famous and many other writers imitated it. The good, middle-class heroine, young Sara, is betrayed by her love Mellefont and poisoned by his girlfriend. Audiences cried tears of pity for Sara's plight. For the first time, because of Lessing's plays, middle class people were attracted to the theater in Germany. Lessing proved that a play on a native subject — something about Germans, not gods or mythical characters — could be successful.

As a result of the foundation laid by Lessing, Neuber, Gottsched, and others, rulers stopped ignoring the public theater in the last quarter of the eighteenth century. Many of the rulers started competing to establish theaters in their provinces. The theater in Germany was now seen as a cultural institution that should be open to all people, and by the 1790s there were more than seventy acting companies. Permanent, state-supported theaters were built. Now actors were held in higher regard and serious, well-written plays had a chance to be accepted.

## A Great Actor, Friedrich Schröder

Friedrich Ludwig Schröder soon built a successful acting company and theater, the National Theatre in Hamburg. Schröder was born into a theatrical family and appeared on stage from the age of three. Child parts were written into plays for him, and when he was a bit older he often played the role of a young girl. The tall and athletic Schröder became Germany's greatest actor and he played more than 700 roles. He introduced the plays of William Shakespeare to German audiences and played many of Shakespeare's most famous roles. Like other individual performers we have met from the eighteenth century, Schröder tried to make each character seem natural.

In spite of Schröder's fame and achievements as actor, director, and manager, he always remained the employee of his mother, Sophie. Schröder worked extremely hard, yet in 1780 his mother paid him the same salary he made in 1771.

## Goethe and Schiller

There were two geniuses in the German theater during the century's final years. Johann Wolfgang von Goethe became interested in the theater at age four when his parents gave him a puppet theater, and Friedrich von Schiller fell in love with literature when he was thirteen. Goethe and Schiller became Germany's greatest playwrights. Schiller was a former army doctor, and Goethe was a lawyer, educator, poet, novelist, scientist, and statesman.

When Goethe was only twenty-four years old he wrote a play that helped start a literary movement. The play was *Götz von Berlichingen* and the movement was called *Sturm und Drang*, or Storm and Stress. In *Götz von Berlichingen* the hero is a German

*Friedrich Ludwig Schröder as Falstaff, in William Shakespeare's* Henry IV (Part I), *1780. Courtesy of The Billy Rose Theatre Collection, The New York Public Library for the Performing Arts, Astor, Lenox and Tilden Foundations.*

outlaw who disobeys the authorities to gain political freedom. His story is told over a period of several years in fifty-six short scenes. The writers of the French neoclassical rules would have been horrified at this Goethe play and at Schiller's play *Die Räuber*, or *The Robbers*.

Schiller started writing *The Robbers* in 1777 when he was eighteen and finished it when he was twenty-two. He wrote *The Robbers* while he was a medical student. Often he had to cover his papers quickly with his medical textbook when the schoolmaster entered his room without warning. Schiller also pretended to be sick so he could go to the infirmary and work on his play. This trick worked until the doctors asked how such a healthy man could be sick so often.

*The Robbers* relates the tragic adventure of Charles von Moor, who becomes the leader of a band of robbers. Von Moor fights against injustice, but his lawlessness leads to the deaths of his father and girlfriend. Finally, when von Moor sees that lawlessness won't bring freedom, he leaves the robbers and gives himself up.

Writers in the Storm and Stress movement were inspired by William Shakespeare's plays, not the French neoclassical works. Instead of characters who were restrained and who reasoned out every action, these writers showed characters who act according to their instincts. Instead of the world being orderly, we see characters struggling in a mysterious world that doesn't make sense. The writers said that society corrupts people who are basically good.

*A scene from* The Robbers *by Friedrich von Schiller. Courtesy Drama Library, Yale University.*

*A scene from a production of* Mary Stuart *by Friedrich von Schiller at The Shakespeare Theatre at the Folger with Monique Fowler as Mary Stuart and Franchelle Stewart Dorn as Queen Elizabeth I. Photograph by Willard Volz. Courtesy of The Shakespeare Theatre at the Folger.*

Ironically, Goethe and Schiller later rejected the Storm and Stress style and instead wrote plays that imitated the works of the ancient Greeks. Schröder wanted to present realistic portrayals of contemporary characters and situations. Goethe and Schiller now argued that plays should portray some higher universal truth and beauty. Their classical dramas became some of the best plays in German theater history. Goethe's masterpiece is *Faust*, which he began writing when he was young and worked on for fifty years. In poetic language Goethe told the legend of Faust, who sells his soul to the devil in return for one moment of pure happiness. Faust learns that pleasures don't make you happy, but work and striving do.

Schiller's historical dramas, including *Mary Stuart, William Tell*, and *The Maid of Orleans*, tell the stories of famous people during a time of crisis in their lives. The plays show how a person's human spirit, his desire for freedom and desire to be true to himself, help him overcome difficult situations. Schiller believed in heroes, people fighting for liberty.

These plays were staged at the Weimar Court Theatre. With Goethe as director and Schiller as playwright, the Weimar Theatre became the cultural and theatrical center of Germany. First, however, Goethe had to take the undereducated actors at Weimar and train them to work as a team. He wanted them to act with dignity and discipline. To get these results Goethe was like a dictator to his company and the players were his puppets. Goethe told the actors how to read and pronounce their lines. He marked the stage off with chalk and drilled the performers over and over in how and where they should move. The actors and actresses were disciplined, if not inspired.

As a result of his work with actors, Goethe published a list of ninety-one rules for players to follow in order to be graceful and dignified in their roles. One rule forbade spitting on stage. Other rules included how actors should pronounce words, move, group themselves, stand, and behave in their private lives. One eighteen-year-old actress from the Weimar company went to Berlin without permission to act in a play. Goethe put her under house arrest for

They said that the nobility creates conditions that force middle-class people to go against their good nature and commit bad deeds. Audiences saw plays on many subjects; for example, the conflict between two brothers who love the same woman or the tale of an unmarried woman who is executed for killing her young child.

The Storm and Stress plays were difficult to stage because they constantly changed scene and journeyed through time. Audiences were confused and shocked by these plays. The young writers were rebelling against established authority and, while their plays were only popular during the 1770s, they did help later playwrights think in new ways.

a week and the actress had to pay for the guard who was stationed at her door.

Goethe even regulated how members of the audience should behave, forbidding them to show approval except by applauding. From his box at the back of the auditorium, Goethe scolded the spectators to be quiet if they didn't like the play. He ordered audience members who misbehaved to be arrested. Goethe was kinder to the children in the audience, whom he sometimes offered cream tarts.

As a result of the efforts of all these individuals, Germany became the leader in the theater by 1800. German theater had come a long way in one century. During the eighteenth century the theaters of many countries influenced each other as plays, players, and production techniques traveled from nation to nation. Acting finally was treated seriously by some performers, and theater people were no longer amateurs, but professionals.

# 4. THE NINETEENTH CENTURY: MELODRAMAS AND WELL-MADE PLAYS

"Don't miss Carlos the dog and his daring rescue."

"Victor Hugo's Hernani incites fights at the Comédie Française."

"See the latest naval battle at Sadler's Wells Theatre."

"Buy tickets now for Edmund Kean in *Henry VIII*. Kean is all violence, all extreme passion."

These are just a few of the advertisements for plays that you might have read in newspapers if you traveled through Europe in the nineteenth century. Even though this was not an era of great plays there was a variety of theatrical entertainment, many theaters in which to see it, and stars, lots of stars. But let's start at the beginning.

## THE ROMANTIC STYLE OF ACTING

The century opened with the stately and dignified acting of Sarah Siddons, her brother John Kemble, and Goethe's performers at Weimar. Soon a new style of acting was popular, the romantic style. The German performer Ludwig Devrient was a typical romantic actor. Devrient, with his long dark hair, pale face, and sad eyes, looked as if he were possessed by intense, passionate emotions. His death scenes were long and drawn out. Romantic actors showed emotion with exaggerated gestures and expressions, opening a letter with trembling hands, crumpling a handkerchief in anger. Eighteenth century actors used their voices; nineteenth century performers used their bodies as well.

### Edmund Kean

The gifted actor Edmund Kean introduced the romantic style in England. Kean was poor and unhappy as a child. Even though he wore leg braces, he was forced to play Cupid at age three because his mother wanted him to earn spending money for her. Later Kean pretended to be a deaf orphan and he ran away

*Edmund Kean in the title role of* Richard III *by William Shakespeare. Courtesy of The Museum of the City of New York.*

to sea.

In 1814 Kean performed at Drury Lane. It was snowing heavily and not many people attended the theater, but Kean was an instant hit. People interrupted his performance with applause. Kean went on to excel in roles that required him to act insane, frenzied, or villainous. He cringed or crawled on the floor to create the right effect. Spectators claimed that when Kean acted angry it was like a hurricane or a tornado, and critics said he was "possessed with a fury, a demon." It is told that during one performance spectators and actors fainted from the power of Kean's acting. Kean was an unstable and self-destructive man who led a wild life, loved many women, and drank heavily.

## George Frederick Cooke

George Frederick Cooke also was English, a romantic actor, and often drunk. When he was sober he was a brilliant performer, especially in villainous roles, but when drunk he was like a maniac and people hissed him off the stage. When Cooke died his body was buried, but a theater company kept his head for its production of *Hamlet*. Eventually, Cooke's head ended up at the New York Phrenological Society. The news reached London and Edmund Kean, who was Cooke's greatest fan, came to New York to bury Cooke's body properly—with his head. Kean did keep one of Cooke's toes as a good luck charm.

## The New Romantic Drama

Romantic performers and acting styles were an outgrowth of the new romantic dramas. Romanticism in playwriting began in Germany and then spread throughout Europe. The romantic writers used Goethe, Schiller, and Shakespeare as their models. They abandoned the rules of the neoclassicists, mixed elements of tragedy and comedy, and wrote stories that rambled through time and place. The romantic writers looked at the world around them and wanted something else, something better. They were tired of revolutions like the French Revolution, and they were weary of wars like the Napoleonic wars. They were sick of rules and the political authorities who controlled their lives.

The romantic writers didn't find meaning in the present, in society, or in civilization. They wanted peace, quiet, a place where everyone could succeed, not just the rich. They believed in individuality, in men relying on their emotions. So their plays escape to the distant past, exotic or foreign locations, to nature or the supernatural. The romanticists used mythology, fairy tales, childhood dreams, or fantasies to fashion plays. The hero in a romantic play might be a rebel, a wanderer, an outcast, or a mysterious stranger. These heroes are sensitive and have a need to give of themselves to love or to a cause. They often stand up for what they believe and suffer greatly or die because of it. For the hero, there is danger, adventure, sacrifice, or heartbreak.

These plays sometimes made a political statement about the state of the world. For example, in 1836 the German playwright Georg Büchner started to write *Woyzech* to show how corrupt humanity is. Like the heroes of many romantic plays, Büchner died young. He died of typhus before he could finish the play.

Romantic plays often took audiences to the Middle Ages and the world of knights, battles, crusades, castles, dungeons, and dark and gloomy forests. There vicious tyrants preyed on innocent victims. When romantic writers did write about the present, the characters were simple folk who lived in the country or some colorful locale like a gypsy camp, a Swiss village, a Sicilian fishing port, or the Alps. The young women were virtuous and the young men heroic and true.

## Romanticism in France

The ideas of the romantic writers aren't revolutionary today but they were for France in 1830. The Comédie Française, the national theater of France, still produced the classic plays written according to the neoclassical rules. The playwright Victor Hugo declared that this obsession with rules and traditions made it impossible for the theater to experiment and grow. He wanted to decide how he should write his plays and he decided to test his ideas.

Hugo wrote a romantic drama, *Hernani*, in twenty-six days and read scenes from it to friends. For weeks before it was staged people argued, debated, and attacked the play in the newspapers. The traditionalists, people who believed dramatists should write plays according to the neoclassical rules, threatened riots and death. Then the first performance of *Hernani* came.

Several hundred of Hugo's supporters arrived midday at the Comédie Française. They were the *claque*. In many European cities, especially in France, Spain, and Italy, theaters had claques—people hired to applaud, to sway the audience's opinion. Often actors or playwrights paid for the claques' seats. On this particular day the Hugo supporters sang, chanted, cheered, ate, and drank wine in the pit and in the upper gallery. When the lamps were lit the auditorium smelled of garlic and sausage. Shortly after the play began, fights broke out and the people who favored tradition tried to boo the play off the stage. The writer Honoré de Balzac was hit in the face by a chunk of cabbage. For forty-five nights the debate continued, but *Hernani* and French romantic drama triumphed.

*Hernani* is the romantic tale of the wild, handsome leader of an outlaw band. Hernani vows revenge on the king, Charles V, who has executed his father and deprived him of his noble inheritance. He races to the castle to rescue his love, Donna Sol, from the old man who plans to marry her and the king who loves her, too. Ultimately, Hernani's adventures bring death to those who join him, and Hernani denounces himself and calls for peace between enemies.

So why were people so upset? In telling Hernani's story Hugo used words considered inappropriate for tragedies and he mixed humor with seriousness. Hugo shocked audiences further by depicting scenes of death and violence on stage. Hugo was a respected writer, and *Hernani* was staged at the home of classical drama in France.

## THE RISE OF MELODRAMA

Ironically, after such a huge battle, the romantic movement in drama didn't last long. A simple version of the romantic drama was the most popular form for most of the nineteenth century. It played in professional theaters in Germany, Russia, and Italy, in the boulevard theaters in France, and it reached its peak in England. It was called *melodrama*.

More and more working class people wanted to be entertained. In England the Industrial Revolution resulted in hordes of factory workers migrating from the country to the cities where the manufacturing jobs were. Large populations meant large potential theater audiences. Melodramas offered what the uneducated working class audiences wanted—escape from their humdrum lives, their poor living conditions, and the turmoil in the world that made them feel threatened and insecure.

German playwright August von Kotzebue wrote many melodramas before he was stabbed to death by a fanatical student. In France René Charles Guilbert de Pixérécourt wrote melodramas for people who couldn't read. Kotzebue's and Pixérécourt's plays

*Theater home of the Comédie Française throughout the nineteenth century. Courtesy Phot. Bibliothèque Nationale, Paris.*

*Scene from a Viennese melodrama, 1829. Courtesy Historisches Museum der Stadt Wien.*

were translated, adapted, and staged in many countries. In melodramas there are good characters and bad characters. The hero or the heroine is pursued by a villain, perhaps a nobleman or a wicked landlord. The villain's schemes to make the hero suffer or to kill the hero, and the hero's attempts to escape threatening predicaments keep the plot going. The audience feared for the good characters and booed the nasty ones. Villains use a variety of tricks to get what they want, but no matter what happens, all ends happily when the hero escapes or is rescued at the last moment and the villain is defeated and punished. The audience always left feeling good that, at least on the stage, justice was handed out the way they felt it should be.

Melodrama means "melody drama" or "play with music." Originally melodramas were plays spoken to background music that expressed the emotions of the scene. Music was used the way it is in movies and television shows today. The hero and the villain also had music to accompany their entrances and exits, and certain instruments were associated with particular characters, such as the trumpet for the hero.

## Amazing Spectacles

Melodramas usually included amazing spectacles like battles, floods, and earthquakes. Often these natural disasters were used to move the plot. In one melodrama a volcano erupts and the villain is destroyed as the lava covers the stage. A flood results in the heroine being carried away to safety on a plank in another play. In *Under the Gaslight* the villain throws the heroine under a dropping elevator, tosses her off a bridge, and ties her to a railroad track in the path of an advancing train before he is defeated and the heroine is saved.

In large theaters across Europe that could hold this spectacular scenery and these special effects, masses of people came to see the latest adventure, and they weren't disappointed. If you saw *The Woodsman's Hut* you would witness the good characters tossed into a river during a violent thunderstorm. Then you would gasp as the heroes dash through the flames of a forest fire set by the villains. Finally, you would watch horrified as they ran safely across a burning bridge, which then collapsed into the river. In *The Streets of London* a real fire engine

*A scene from* Under the Gaslight *by Augustin Daly. Courtesy University of Bristol, England.*

with bells ringing rushes onto the stage at the climax. Audiences saw glowing embers, walls cracking with heat, charred rafters crashing, and blazing flames.

Audiences witnessed many marvels, such as trees bending in the wind or the avalanche in *Pauvrette* that trapped the hero and the heroine in a hut. Some theaters had reservoirs of water under the stage for nautical melodramas. In these plays ships floated and sometimes blew up and sank. Women and children were saved from drowning. In *The Loss of the Royal George* sailors were seen swimming in the water, and in *Formosa* a boat race was rowed. The Sadler's Wells Theatre in London was famous for its water tank in which naval battles between model ships were enacted.

As new technology became available it was used in the theater for some mechanical wonder. When electricity was invented later in the century theater

engineers fashioned treadmills powered by electric motors to stage horse or chariot races. Real horses ran on the treadmills while a *panorama* rolled past. The panorama was a long cloth on which a continuous scene was painted. It was attached at either side of the stage to giant spools, and when it was rolled behind the running horses, it looked like the horses were racing around a track.

## Dogs and Children, Too

People liked novelty and this led to some unusual entertainment. Dog dramas were a hit. At Drury Lane in London audiences cheered when the dog Carlos rescued a heroine from a tank of water. Pixérécourt's play *The Dog of Montargis* starred a dog, too. There were riots in Dublin, Ireland when the dog was missing for two weeks. Philip Astley in England attracted crowds to his Astley's Circus for equestrian spectacles, dramas featuring horses. Audiences

*Ellen Bateman as Richard III and Kate Bateman as Richmond. Engraving by Hollis, from a daguerreotype by Mayall. Reproduced by permission of The Huntington Library, San Marino, California.*

*William Henry West Betty, at age thirteen. Courtesy Harvard Theatre Collection.*

witnessed battles and sieges involving squadrons of horsemen.

Child performers, often called "Infant Prodigies," were popular with audiences during the nineteenth century, and for a short time they enjoyed more attention than rock stars do today. One young lady known as "Miss Mudie" debuted in London at Covent Garden when she was eight. Audiences raved about her until she appeared as a wife in one play; they couldn't accept a little girl as a wife. Kate and Ellen Bateman from America charmed audiences in London during several tours. They first appeared on the London stage when Kate was eight and Ellen was seven and performed female and male roles in several of Shakespeare's plays.

The most famous child star was William Henry West Betty of England. A tiny, slim boy, Betty performed leading roles, including many tragic characters, at the age of thirteen. The royal family praised him, poetry was written in his honor, and pictures of him sold throughout England. On one occasion the prime minister adjourned the House of Commons so its members could watch Betty perform. Unfortunately, within a few years people hissed him off the stage. He did retire from the theater in his teens with a fortune, but his father squandered his money and the rest of Betty's life was uneventful.

## MUSIC HALLS

Working class audiences in England and in France liked entertainment that offered them fun and a good time at a low cost. Theater managers, who had no connection to the theater other than as a commercial venture, were happy to supply such entertainment. They could bring in the crowds and make lots of money.

Music halls sprang up all over England in the mid- and late nineteenth century. At first, a music hall was a room attached to a tavern so people could drink and be entertained. Later, music halls were large theaters in which audiences enjoyed short plays and specialty acts by different performers: dancers, comedians, jugglers, and singers. Outside of England cafés and cabarets offered similar entertainment.

## DRAMA AROUND EUROPE

Few noteworthy plays were written in the early and mid-nineteenth century, but a few writers experimented. Some young writers protested against the theater's obsession with melodrama and spectacle. In Germany political control led to uninspired theater, yet some young playwrights wrote controversial plays that often got them into trouble with the censors. These playwrights, including Friedrich Hebbel, wrote about social causes and contemporary problems. Their plays were more realistic than anything previously written and were virtually unknown until the twentieth century.

Russia also had strict censorship under the Czars Nicholas I and Nicholas II and their secret police, but some fine writers developed, such as Ivan Turgenev. In his play *A Month in the Country*, he focused on the characters instead of the unfolding story. He wrote characters who underneath a quiet surface are leading unhappy lives. Nikolai Gogol penned *The Inspector General*, a wonderful satire on corruption among political officials. By some miracle the Czar

*A scene from* La dame aux camélias *by Alexandre Dumas fils at the Théâtre de Paris. Courtesy French Cultural Services.*

liked it so it was allowed to be staged.

In France Alexandre Dumas fils and Emile Augier wrote plays about middle-class people, social dramas that dealt with contemporary problems. Their themes included corruption in politics, religious prejudice, and disreputable journalism. Their purpose was to moralize, correct misbehavior, and enforce middle class virtues. The public wasn't crazy about most of their plays, but *La Dame aux Camélias* by Dumas fils was popular for decades. It offered actresses a great leading role. La Dame aux Camélias is a courtesan, a lady of easy virtue, who reforms but dies in her lover's arms. Dumas fils treated her character sympathetically.

## Eugene Scribe's "Well-Made Plays"

These plays from Germany, Russia, and France were often praised by critics, but people who were going to the theater to relax and be amused preferred the plays of Eugene Scribe of France. From 1839 to 1860 Scribe was the most popular playwright. He wrote stories about contemporary society, often about middle-class families. Scribe didn't write about controversial subjects. In Scribe's plays wives always win back their husbands, and parents always succeed with their children. The characters are always secure—women in their marriage and home, citizens in their state and business. The characters in these plays don't behave the way real human beings do and the situations are trivial and improbable.

Scribe's plays are complicated, carefully worked out stories that keep the audience in suspense and hold their attention. He used a variety of startling situations and intrigues to keep the plays going. The audience might wait for a secret to be uncovered or someone's identity might be revealed by a birthmark. A confidential letter might be hidden or dropped in public and then discovered at the appropriate moment. In some plays a goblet of poisoned wine might pass from person to person until it is drunk by someone other than the intended victim.

Scribe's plays were so carefully constructed that they were called "well-made plays." Scribe had developed a formula for writing plays of all types. He even developed a "play factory," consisting of many writers, each of whom wrote a specific part of each

play. Later writers would use Scribe's play form to write about important ideas. Victorien Sardou followed Scribe, used his well-made play formula to write all kinds of plays, and was the second most popular playwright of the second half of the century.

## Dion Boucicault

Irishman Dion Boucicault was the most successful playwright in England during this period. Most of his plays were "native melodramas," set in contemporary England, and each usually had a "sensation scene"—some novel and spectacular effect. In *The Octoroon* a steamboat explodes, and in *The Colleen Baun* there is an attempted drowning.

Boucicault was also the first playwright to demand and get a royalty—a share of the profits—for

*Dion Boucicault in* The Shaughraun. *Courtesy Drama Library, Yale University.*

each performance of his plays. Until this time authors would sell their plays outright to a manager for a low fee. They had to write twenty to thirty plays every year to survive. There were also many managers who would plagiarize material. They would send a hired underling to a competing theater to make a copy of the play that was being shown there. Then the manager would stage the same work in his theater.

## THE "STAR SYSTEM"

Another aspect of the nineteenth century theater was the "star system" that came to dominate the acting profession. Individual talented performers were featured in plays, and the other players were subordinate to them. The star would tour different theaters with two or three supporting actors, and the theaters they visited would stage the play and provide the rest of the performers. The play and the performance suffered because everyone didn't rehearse together, but this practice brought in the crowds to see the stars.

As costs of productions went up and the performers', especially the stars', salaries went up, only the "long run" of a play was profitable—keeping a production going for as long as there were audiences, instead of changing the play every night. The commercial theaters only staged plays they knew would be popular and make money.

Another result, especially in England, was fewer permanent companies of actors that had been in existence since Shakespearean times. Instead of playing in each production a theater staged, actors often were hired for a single play. Consequently, actors played fewer roles and had less opportunity to grow as performers.

There were many outstanding actors and actresses during this period, including Ludwig Devrient and Edmund Kean whom we have already met. Most performers began acting as children and many belonged to acting families. The best players brought fine acting to all types of plays—tragedies, domestic plays, comedies—whether the dramas were good or bad. For the most part, they acted on instinct, not trying to interpret their characters, just trying to arouse people's emotions.

There were handbooks written on the art of acting that told an actor or actress how to pose, how to project his voice, and how to arrange himself in relation to other people on stage. Some performers tried to act more naturally, but for many performers acting still was something artificial, stylized—from the way they spoke and moved to the way they held their pose and gestured.

## Three French Actresses

Three outstanding actresses came from France. Rachel (Éliza Félix) was a poor child who began her career as a street singer when she was thirteen. A kind soul saw her and sent her to drama school, but her father yanked her from school to start performing. At age fourteen Rachel played the role of Juliet in Shakespeare's *Romeo and Juliet* and she went on to star in classical and Shakespearean roles.

Eleanora Duse was born in a third class railroad car while her parents were traveling with the Duse family troupe to perform in Milan, Italy. Duse acted on stage when she was four and by twelve she was performing regularly, often playing characters much older than herself. When she was twenty, Duse had to replace a leading actress at the last moment and she was a hit. Duse matured into a sad, expressive, and beautiful woman, slender and graceful. She became internationally famous and was admired in tragedies and big emotional parts. Duse refused to wear makeup on stage and lived a reclusive life.

For the ultimate star no one outshone the "Divine Sarah." Sarah Bernhardt assembled her own troupes and took her plays to theaters throughout Europe. No matter where she performed, Bernhardt spoke in French. She starred in tragic and Shakespearean roles, but she always played herself and was more a personality than an actress. Bernhardt's aim was to be unusual, to shock, astonish, and amaze people. She was a beautiful, slim, dark-eyed woman, and she had a magnetism that attracted people. Bernhardt became a legend and like other stars, people came to see her, no matter what the play was. "Divine Sarah" was also eccentric. She slept in a coffin and supposedly demanded payment in gold for her performances. When Bernhardt was seventy-

*Rachel as Rosalana in* Bajazet. *Reproduced by permission of The Huntington Library, San Marino, California.*

one years old she reappeared on stage despite having recently had her leg amputated.

## Other Actors and Actresses

There were other stars, like Helena Modjeska in Poland. From Italy came Adelaide Ristori and Tommaso Salvini, who, like the French actresses above, toured the world. Ristori, another child of actors, was first carried on stage in a basket at the age of two months. Ristori appeared in many infant roles and beginning when she was four, she played children's parts. Ristori started playing leading tragic roles at age fifteen. Tommaso Salvini began his theatrical career when he was fourteen. Salvini is said to have had an inner fire and to have terrified his leading ladies because his acting was so intense.

In England, besides Edmund Kean, William Charles Macready ushered in the romantic acting style. He was ideal for romantic roles — thin and pale with high cheekbones, dark hair, and brown eyes. His behavior in one particular play reveals his style and temperament. Macready's servant was supposed to be in the wings of the theater with a bowl of cochineal, a bright red liquid, which Macready needed to smear on his hands to look like blood. The servant was not there and Macready only had a few moments before he had to walk on stage again. While he was in the wings, he punched a man in the nose and smeared his hands with the flowing blood. Macready went on stage, finished the performance, and then apologized to the man he had punched.

*William Charles Macready in the title role of* Macbeth *by William Shakespeare. Courtesy Drama Library, Yale University.*

Hot-tempered Macready never intended to be an actor, but he was forced out of school and into the theater to pay his father's debts. Macready always said that he hated being an actor. He was ashamed of his profession and disgusted by the conditions he saw. In spite of his feelings, Macready devoted himself to the theater. He tried to make theaters respectable places and he cleared them of undesirables.

## ACTOR-MANAGERS

Macready and Edmund Kean were among several performers in England who were part of another important facet of nineteenth century theater, the actor-manager. Actor-managers ran their own theaters, hired the performers, and staged and starred in plays they selected or that were written for them. Some actor-managers were egocentric. Most preferred to present spectacles and to showcase the talents of a few chosen players, especially themselves. Often their chief goal was to get the actors to the theater sober, in time for a show, and knowing their lines.

### Madame Vestris

Some actor-managers did try to improve the state of the theater. One of the most noted and respected actress-managers was Madame Vestris (Lucia Elizabetta Bartolozzi Mathews). Vestris's management of a theater was bold at the time because it was unheard of for a woman. But this intelligent woman purchased a small disreputable playhouse and turned it into an intimate, fashionable theater—the Olympic Theatre, where a more refined audience felt welcome. Vestris staged "light entertainment" including comedies and "domestic dramas." She kept discipline among her players and introduced varied and appropriate costuming for the time and the characters.

Madame Vestris also is credited with making the "box set" popular. The sides or flats of the stage were closed in to form a room with real walls. This was a more realistic alternative to the system of painted wings and shutters, hanging borders, and backcloths, which had been used since the Italian

Renaissance. With the wing system, every detail was painted on canvas, including doors, windows, draperies, and furniture. Vestris furnished her box sets like rooms in real homes with rugs and bookcases, tables and chairs. She used heavy moldings, real windows and doors with doorknobs, even ceilings. If acting was not yet lifelike, the picture—costumes, props, and sets—was becoming very realistic.

### Squire Bancroft and Marie Wilton

Like Madame Vestris, Squire Bancroft and his wife Marie Wilton, a popular actress, took over the management of a disused and seedy theater known as the "Dust Hole." The Bancrofts refurbished the theater and put in something new—comfortable blue velvet "stall" seats, seats in the pit instead of benches. They even carpeted the area. The Bancrofts also wanted an intimate theater that would attract the now powerful and influential middle class.

*Squire Bancroft as Triplet in* Masks and Faces *by Tom Taylor. Courtesy Drama Library, Yale University.*

## NEW THEATERS AND NEW PLAYWRIGHTS IN ENGLAND

Everywhere in England there were new, smaller, more expensive playhouses that attracted middle- and upper-class audiences. Here the pit was pushed to the back and provided with only a few rows of benches. The rest of the area between the pit and the stage was now called the "stalls" or "orchestra stalls" and was filled with comfortable seats, which became the best and most expensive seats to buy. The seats were numbered and could be reserved in advance, more like the playhouses of today. These theaters opened later in the evening and offered all types of plays because the Theatre Act of 1843 had given all English theaters permission to produce plays. In these small, fashionable theaters, audiences enjoyed cleaner, more comfortable, and better ventilated auditoriums than the crowds who attended the large theaters to watch melodramas and spectacles. The audience looked quite elegant in their evening dress—the men in white ties, the women in diamonds.

### Tom Robertson

In these intimate theaters, audiences enjoyed plays like those of Englishman Tom Robertson, who came from a family of twenty-two children and wrote plays for the Bancrofts' theater. Robertson tried to avoid wildly dramatic scenes, huge flowery speeches, and

*Marie Bancroft and John Hare in* Caste *by Tom Robertson. Courtesy The Raymond Mander and Joe Mitchenson Theatre Collection Ltd.*

unreal characters in unlikely situations. He wrote plays about contemporary life, humorous drama about ordinary people. His plays, including *Society, Caste,* and *Home* were called "cup and saucer dramas" because Robertson used all sorts of little incidents to give real-life touches to his scenes. In *Caste* there is a kitchen tea party scene in which the characters pour tea, spoon in sugar, stir the tea, and take great care in all the activities associated with drinking tea. Robertson also insisted on setting his plays in realistic rooms, so he used the box set and filled the scene with pictures, ornaments, clocks, and furniture.

## Other Playwrights

Toward the end of the century in England the intimate playhouses with red velvet curtains and glittering chandeliers moved on. They saw the dramas about life and love in fashionable society of Sir Arthur Pinero and the comedies of Henry Arthur Jones. Audiences would also enjoy the musical comedies of W.S. Gilbert, which satirize the times, like *H.M.S. Pinafore*, which was disrespectful to the British navy. Oscar Wilde sparkled with his brilliant, witty comedies. Wilde's most famous play, which is often performed today, is *The Importance of Being Earnest*. It is an entertaining play full of fun and nonsense, preposterous situations, and witty dialogue where trivial matters are treated seriously. Underneath, Wilde poked fun and ridiculed the social hypocrisy he saw in the Victorian society in which he lived.

## SHAKESPEARE REDISCOVERED

One playwright was rediscovered during the nineteenth century, William Shakespeare. It was in that century that he gained his reputation as the greatest dramatist of all time. His plays continued to offer many leading actors and actresses their most challenging roles. Some actor-managers, like William Charles Macready, produced Shakespeare's plays according to the original text, with the scenes complete and in the proper order. Since the seventeenth century Shakespeare's plays had been mangled, rearranged, and rewritten.

Other actor-managers, such as Sir Herbert

*A scene from Arizona Theatre Company's 1990 production of* The Importance of Being Earnest *by Oscar Wilde, with Tom Harrison and Francia DiMase. Photograph by Tim Fuller. Courtesy Arizona Theatre Company.*

Beerbohm Tree, turned Shakespeare's plays into lavish historical spectacles. In *The Tempest* Beerbohm Tree had a ship rocking in a sea with waves splashing over the deck. In *A Midsummer Night's Dream* the scene of the woods near Athens, Greece had live rabbits running around and a carpet of grass with flowers that could be plucked. Beerbohm Tree also left his mark on the English theater by establishing an acting school in 1904, which would become the Royal Academy of Dramatic Art (RADA), still the most prestigious acting school in England.

Shakespeare's plays are set in many different time periods and provided wonderful opportunities for actor-managers who strived for historical accuracy in their plays. Charles Kean, son of Edmund Kean, was an actor-manager who took so much stock in historical accuracy that he sent scene painters to

*Scene from Beerbohm Tree's production of* A Midsummer Night's Dream *by William Shakespeare. Courtesy of the Board of Trustees of the Victoria and Albert Museum.*

*Ellen Terry as Beatrice in* Much Ado About Nothing *by William Shakespeare. Courtesy Drama Library, Yale University.*

Rome and Athens to sketch the landscape, then reproduce their subjects on stage. Kean researched various periods by studying ancient records and old prints. In his production of Shakespeare's *King John* Kean attempted to reproduce authentic medieval costumes. On one occasion Kean provided the audience with a list of authorities he had consulted in his search for historical accuracy.

## HENRY IRVING

Henry Irving also spent enormous sums on his lavish productions with settings so realistic it was like looking at a three-dimensional photograph. For Goethe's *Faust* he had the swords used in a duel scene electrically wired so that flashes of electricity appeared whenever the swords met. Audiences loved this type of realism. A member of the audience once wrote to Irving and offered her baby as a replacement for the doll used in Shakespeare's *Henry III* so the audience wouldn't laugh when Irving kissed it.

Irving is considered the greatest actor-manager in England during the nineteenth century. He attracted talented performers to his Lyceum Theatre, including his leading lady for twenty-five years, Ellen Terry. Terry first performed at age ten and in her youth endured lengthy rehearsals that often lasted until four or five a.m. Her legs ached and sometimes Terry could hardly keep her eyes open on stage. She became a slender, graceful leading lady who was loved by audiences.

Irving was internationally famous. He, like Madame Vestris and William Charles Macready, attracted educated and refined middle-class audiences, and devoted time to the details of his productions of Shakespeare and contemporary melodramas. In 1895 Irving became the first performer in England to be knighted for his work in the theater. He accepted the honor on behalf of the whole theater profession, which had so often been slandered and considered idle and drunken. Until 1824 actors were officially classified as "rogues and vagabonds" in England. With this honor, performers were accepted in high society.

## NEW REALISM ON STAGE

### Makeup

Advances in science and technology made it easier for the actor-managers to achieve the realistic picture on stage they wanted. Modern theatrical makeup was invented toward the end of the century. Instead of powders, especially white powder made from poisonous lead, actors now used grease paint. It was made in many colors from light flesh color to reddish brown and packaged in round sticks. This is essentially the same makeup performers use today. The only difference is that now performers remove grease paint with creams and in the nineteenth century players removed it with cocoa butter.

### Lighting

Advances in methods of lighting affected the theater, too. During the 1800s gaslight was introduced in theaters. Gas smelled awful and over four hundred theaters burned down because of the open jets of flame, but gas was more efficient than candles and lamp light. The flow of gas could be controlled so the lights could be dimmed, put out, or relit. For the first time the auditorium could be darkened and the light concentrated on the stage. Spectators could almost forget about themselves and concentrate on the stage, where the action and the actors were well lit.

Later limelight was developed. This was a type of extremely bright spotlight that could focus attention on a certain acting area or character. From it we get the phrase "in the limelight," which came to refer to stars who usually had the light focused on them. In the 1880s electricity was invented and electric lighting was introduced in theaters. It was safer and easier to control.

## THE EVOLUTION OF ACTING

By the end of the century the stage picture was realistic in the theater even if the plays were not. It remained for others to write plays with characters who spoke and acted naturally, with events that happened believably as they would in real life. Now and again actor-managers attempted having the performers work together as an ensemble to create the play but, generally, acting was a display of individual talent. There were few rehearsals and the actors mainly learned where they would stand, enter the stage, and exit the stage. It was assumed that a performer knew what to do on stage the rest of the time. It was also assumed that when an actor was given his script he would memorize his lines. Some managers attempted long and careful rehearsals and aimed for historical accuracy in costumes and sets, but often the costumes and scenery were not consistent with a historical period.

## The Meiningen Players

A small troupe of actors from Germany combined many elements that we find in the modern theater and showed them to the rest of the world. They were the Meiningen Players and they were directed by George II, Duke of Saxe-Meiningen, ruler of the small German state. The Duke conducted long, disciplined, and careful rehearsals for all roles, large and small. With his wife Ellen Franz he persuaded his performers to work together as an ensemble to achieve a unified stage picture. The chief actors played small parts as well as big ones; there were no stars. Each play had its own individual settings, costumes, and properties, which were accurate for the period and locale in which the play was set. Each actor was given written instructions for wearing his costume.

The Duke's plays were noted for their crowd scenes. The crowds were divided into small groups and each one was headed by an able actor. The Duke designed all aspects of the production himself, including how the actors would move, because he believed in the unifying power of one person in charge of all the aspects of a production. From 1874 to 1890 he took his troupe on extensive tours of Europe from London to Moscow, and his unified effects are what most impressed people. He inspired the fathers of realism including André Antoine and Konstantin Stanislavsky, whom we shall meet shortly.

*A performance of William Shakespeare's* Julius Caesar *by the Saxe-Meiningen Players in London 1881 from the* Illustrated London News. *Courtesy Drama Library, Yale University.*

# 5. MODERN THEATER DAWNS: REALISM AND INDEPENDENT THEATERS

Throughout the nineteenth century, if you were a theater lover, you could visit commercial and state-supported theaters throughout Europe and enjoy entertaining plays. Here and there you would see something a little different—actors trying to work together, at least acting in the same style; plays depicting contemporary characters and problems. In general, though, most productions were lavish and costly, and audiences came to see the stars. Plays, even if they dealt with everyday life and problems, concentrated on supporting existing values in society. Dramas weren't really concerned with what characters were thinking or feeling, but with what characters were doing.

Audiences were used to plays with lots of action and stereotyped characters. They liked these comfortable, predictable plays. If you were an unknown playwright and you wanted to have your play staged, you wrote in a way that you knew would please people. You also wrote plays that passed the inspection of government censors, who banned anything they felt was controversial.

Even though some actor-managers used realistic box sets, many theaters still used scenery that consisted of a few painted sets that were used over and over. Acting, which in a few theaters looked like everyday life, in most theaters was very unrealistic. A performer concentrated on projecting his voice and pronouncing his words carefully. He posed, using specific positions for his hands, feet, head, and torso and used specific facial expressions for different emotions like laughter, fear, love, and pain. Actors, as they had been for several centuries, were hired for "lines of business," a small number of character types that they could perform in all plays. Rarely did an actor think about how the other performers were acting. He was on stage to play his individual part without regard for how it related to the roles of the other actors.

## THE BIRTH OF REALISM

From the 1880s, however, the theater witnessed a rebirth. An independent theater movement grew because some people were dissatisfied with existing theater practices. They revolted against a theater they felt ignored everyday life. These people had exciting new ideas that led to realism in playwriting, acting, and production methods. Realism in the theater came to include scenery that consisted of recognizable surroundings in box sets. The stories were probable, with characters from everyday life who were treated truthfully, not in an idealized way. Acting came to be based on the way people really talk and behave. Important social issues and other new topics were explored in the new realistic plays.

There were few experimenters at first and they were courageous and determined people. Many were amateurs and most worked outside the commercial or state-supported theaters. Commercial theater managers would not present realistic drama because they didn't want to upset their middle-class audiences who were content with theater that entertained. These managers didn't want to stage anything controversial that might disturb and scare away their audiences and the money they spent.

You might think that realism in playwriting would come from a country with a developed theater like Germany or England. Instead, it came from Norway, Sweden, and Russia. These were countries with no strong theatrical traditions where theater artists felt freer to change existing conditions.

## IBSEN, THE FATHER OF REALISM

In Norway Henrik Ibsen was born into a poor family. He didn't read much and he quit school when he was fifteen. Ibsen struggled and faced disappointments, but eventually he became a stage manager at a state

*A scene from Henrik Ibsen's* A Doll's House, *Birmingham Repertory Theatre, Birmingham, England, 1914. Courtesy Drama Library, Yale University.*

theater. There he learned about all the facets of theater production and how to write plays.

In 1879 Ibsen shocked the world with his play *A Doll's House*. In it audiences met Nora, a wife, who realizes that she has been treated like a plaything by her husband and her father. Nora decides that the only way she can be independent, to think and act for herself, is to leave her husband and children. The play was seen as an attack on how society said marriages and families should be, with women responsible for keeping the family happy. In *Ghosts* Ibsen shows another troubled family. A woman stays married to a depraved husband because society says it is her duty to do so. The woman's decision leads to her son Oswald inheriting a venereal disease and losing his mind from it.

## Critics Denounced Him

None of Ibsen's realistic plays have typical, happy endings, nor do they provide solutions to problems. Members of the clergy damned Ibsen. Theaters banned and governments censored his plays. Some theater managers refused to stage *A Doll's House* unless Ibsen wrote a happy ending that kept Nora at home. No Scandinavian theater would produce *Ghosts*. When it was staged in London the reviewers described it as "morbid, unhealthy, unwholesome, and disgusting." When Ibsen's plays were introduced in the United States critics exclaimed that he would disrupt society. Some called his plays "an open drain" and declared that Ibsen would "upend the theater's simple purpose."

When Ibsen started writing, plays were meant to entertain, to make people forget real life. Few people thought of the theater as a place for serious thought. Ibsen was different. He believed that plays could change people and eventually change the moral and social values in society that he felt needed to be challenged.

## Controversial Subjects and Characters

Ibsen wasn't afraid to explore life's serious problems, to tackle subjects considered taboo on stage like the death of a child and hereditary disease. He exposed the lies, hypocrisy, greed, and meanness he found in society. In *The Pillars of Society* he uncovered the unethical practices of shipbuilders, and in *The League of Youth* he exposed the corruption of local politics. In *An Enemy of the People* a Doctor Stockman discovers that the waters in the local spa are polluted and may threaten people's lives. Instead of thanking him, the townspeople condemn him. They wanted to suppress the truth so tourists would come to the spa and make the town rich.

Ibsen knew that his plays would alarm people. In his plays he is saying that everything isn't as wonderful as it appears; all people aren't happy, marriages don't always work, politicians aren't always honest. Ibsen felt that if he didn't disturb people there would have been no need to write his plays.

Always Ibsen asks the question, "How can a person become a true human being?" He felt that individuals needed to find their own freedom and happiness in spite of society trying to make them conform to traditions, conventions, and values. Ibsen challenged the rules of anything that might make people unhappy: marriage, religion, ethics, and morality. Ibsen was a champion of women. He saw how society dictated that women marry and suppress their own wants and desires while concentrating on making their families happy.

Ibsen had an ability to understand human beings, their strivings and failings. He showed the weaknesses and strengths of his characters on stage. No character is all good or all bad. Each character in Ibsen's plays is a personality who behaves the way he does because of some trait inherited from a family member or because of something in his social environment.

## A Model and a Vision

Henrik Ibsen provided a model for writers of realism. His characters live in the here and now. They aren't larger-than-life heroes involved in great adventures. They are ordinary people wrestling with the problems people face. Instead of concentrating on the plot and what happens next, audiences were challenged to observe the characters and to think about the ideas presented. The characters in Ibsen's plays reveal themselves as they would in real life, through their words and actions, and their words sound like ordinary conversation.

Ibsen faced hostility. He struggled with heavy debts. Often he was depressed. But Ibsen gave playwrights a new vision of their role. He had champions, talented people who insisted on staging his plays.

Ibsen showed that drama could reveal insights, impart ideas, and stimulate discussion. To him we give the title "Father of the Modern Drama." His plays have been translated into many languages and are still staged worldwide.

## AUGUST STRINDBERG

In Sweden another playwright would develop about the same time as Ibsen, and he would have as great and as shocking an impact on twentieth century theater. He was August Strindberg. He was born in poverty in Stockholm, Sweden, an unwanted, unloved child who lived in three rooms with ten people. When he was eighteen he went to university, where he froze and went hungry in a tiny attic space. For much of his life Strindberg was close to a mental breakdown. He spent time in hospitals and prisons

*A scene from August Strindberg's play* The Father. *Courtesy Swedish Information Service.*

and dabbled in the occult and black magic. Strindberg, however, did find his strength and salvation in writing.

## Revolt Against Society

Like Ibsen, Strindberg challenged the existing culture and examined the moral values people were supposed to uphold and the social conventions by which they were supposed to live. In his realistic plays he wrote about people's sins and abnormal behavior. He also wrote about the struggle for power between men and women. In *Miss Julie* Strindberg describes the tragedy of a woman in love with a man who is beneath her social class. At the time Strindberg wrote this play, such a situation was unacceptable in society, no matter what the individuals involved thought or felt.

In *The Father* audiences watched as a man was mentally destroyed by the women in his life. At the end of the play, the man's childhood nurse comforts him as she straps him into a straitjacket. When this scene played in a theater in Copenhagen, Denmark, it is said that the audience jumped out of their seats and ran from the theater bellowing like mad bulls. Strindberg shocked people by revealing what was really going on in people's minds.

## FRENCH PLAYWRIGHTS AND NATURALISM

While Ibsen and Strindberg were writing their plays, Émile Zola and other French playwrights were demanding a new drama. It became known as *naturalism*. Zola was influenced by new scientific discoveries and theories, especially those of Charles Darwin. Darwin wrote that people's heredity, their ancestors, and their environment, the society in which they lived—these factors are responsible for how a person develops and behaves more than the person himself is.

## Emile Zola

Zola wanted to turn the stage into a laboratory where life could be studied as it is. He would reproduce a specific environment and show characters struggling in this world. It would be like transferring a piece of reality or a "slice of life" to the stage. In this way the problems of society could be examined, criticized, and changed. Nothing was to be altered or "prettied-up," nothing was left unsaid, so these plays showed all of human experience, usually the sordid and the ugly, the poor and the painful. They tended to be pessimistic plays about how the deprived lower classes—workers, peasants, thieves, prostitutes—were victimized by society. Writers of naturalism wrote plays that were like unedited videotapes of today.

Émile Zola wrote the naturalistic play *Thérèse Raquin* in which Thérèse and her lover drown her husband. The couple are overcome by guilt and they commit suicide. The play was hissed off the stage, and in 1874 Zola qualified to attend the monthly "Dinner for Hissed Authors." Critics exclaimed, "This fellow, Zola, makes one a little sick." Despite the threat of this type of criticism, we will meet other playwrights—Leo Tolstoy, Maxim Gorky, and Gerhart Hauptmann—who wrote naturalistic dramas.

## André Antoine

Zola's ideas also had a great influence on André Antoine of France, who as a youth loved literature and the theater and often went hungry so he could buy theater tickets. In 1887 this unknown clerk who worked in a Paris gas company, this frustrated actor, created the first great experimental theater. With the little money he had Antoine rented a room in a pool hall behind a wine store. He borrowed his mother's furniture and hauled it across Paris. Antoine's theater, the Théâtre Libre (Free Theater) was so small that the audience could shake hands with the actors across the footlights.

Antoine created the Théâtre Libre to present the plays of Ibsen and other realist dramatists. These playwrights could not get their plays produced in commercial theaters because the subjects were controversial and treated realistically. Young, talented authors who might never have written plays did so because the Théâtre Libre was there for them. To avoid censorship Antoine ran his theater privately. He wrote and hand-delivered 1,300 invitations. From the responses he built a list of members who attended his theater for a fee.

*The set for André Antoine's production of Gerhart Hauptmann's* The Weavers. *Courtesy of The Billy Rose Theatre Collection, The New York Public Library for the Performing Arts, Astor, Lenox and Tilden Foundations.*

## Realistic Plays and Production Styles

Other dramatists had written realistic plays in the 1800s but production styles were not realistic and censorship kept the plays from being produced. The Duke of Saxe-Meiningen used some realistic techniques, but he staged melodramas and romantic plays. Antoine was the first to bring realistic plays and realistic production styles together. He produced Ibsen's plays and other plays considered shocking.

Antoine brought a "slice of life" onto the stage by reproducing every detail of a specific environment. The setting was meant to be a place in which the characters live, a force that affects their action and behavior, not just a background. Antoine used real furniture with nicks and stains and rooms arranged as in everyday life. A banquet scene in one show featured roasting geese and real barrels of wine. For the play *Old Heidelberg* Antoine bought a college student's dormitory room and moved it to the stage. In *The Butchers* carcasses of beef were hung on hooks for the butcher shop scene, and real chickens clucked and scurried across the stage.

## New Acting Techniques

Antoine also instituted a new approach to French acting. His performers, including a traveling salesman, a chemist, and a dressmaker, were amateurs who worked days in offices or shops and could rehearse only at night. Antoine instructed them to speak and move as if the characters they played were real people. He urged them to use simple gestures and natural movements. Antoine encouraged them to speak in low voices, to speak while walking or sitting, not just while standing still, and to turn their backs to the audience.

Antoine's theater finally closed because of financial problems, but not before Antoine had become famous worldwide. Antoine showed the world what the theater can do when it is not concerned with traditions and big profits. He influenced actors, producers, and writers, and his example of an independent theater was followed all over Europe.

## GERMAN THEATER

In Berlin, Germany, the director and dramatic critic Otto Brahm became chairman of the Freie Bühne

(Free Stage), a group of ten theater enthusiasts. The Freie Bühne convinced open-minded theater managers to volunteer their buildings and performers on Sundays for private performances of new plays on controversial issues. Because the plays were financed through subscription tickets for private audiences, police could not stop the performances. Brahm hoped that when he showed the merit of these new plays, managers of commercial theaters would stage the plays or later works by the writers.

### Gerhart Hauptmann

The Freie Bühne staged the early plays of Germany's first important playwright of the twentieth century, Gerhart Hauptmann, who wrote about forty plays. His most famous is *The Weavers*, which portrays the revolt of poor and miserable weavers who rise, unsuccessfully, against their employers whom the weavers consider responsible for their suffering.

Hauptmann introduced something new. Instead of an individual as the play's hero, a group is the central character. When the commercial theater, Theatre Deutsches, of Berlin accepted one of Hauptmann's plays, the Freie Bühne was no longer needed.

## ENGLISH THEATER

In 1891 Jacob Thomas Grein founded the Independent Theatre Society in London, England. This organization introduced the plays of Ibsen and new foreign plays to the English public. Its members also hoped to discover and nurture new English playwrights. Unfortunately, when Grein advertised for new plays by English actors, plays that had been suppressed by managers, no one responded. English playwriting was at a low point and there were no new English plays worth producing.

*Scene from a 1928 production at the Guild Theatre, New York of* Major Barbara *by George Bernard Shaw. Courtesy of The Billy Rose Theatre Collection, The New York Public Library for the Performing Arts, Astor, Lenox and Tilden Foundations.*

*A scene from a 1989 Pioneer Theatre Company production of* Saint Joan *by George Bernard Shaw. Courtesy Pioneer Theatre Company.*

## George Bernard Shaw

Grein encouraged George Bernard Shaw to write a play. This play, *Widower's House*, was the first of many that ultimately saw Shaw labeled the "father of the theater of ideas." Shaw was a crusader who thought plays were a more effective way to distribute his ideas than presenting a speech or handing out pamphlets. He felt a need to criticize existing social, political, and moral traditions in the hopes of correcting them.

Shaw exposed slum landlords in *Widower's House* and the tragedy of war in *Arms and the Man*. In *Pygmalion* Professor Higgins, a speech professor, changes the speech of an ignorant Cockney girl so she can fake her way into aristocratic society. Shaw was showing the foolishness of distinctions between different social classes. In 1956 *Pygmalion* was adapted into the popular American musical *My Fair Lady*.

Shaw wanted the public to face up to unpleasant facts about society and institutions. He saw issues from many sides and he explored them in depth. In *Major Barbara* the title character works for the Salvation Army and gives food and clothes to the poor. Her father runs a munitions factory, which manufactures guns and other weapons that kill people in war. But the factory employs the poor and provides them with a paycheck. By the end of the play the father seems the better person.

Shaw's plays are full of talk and little action, and his themes are serious. Shaw also wanted to entertain audiences, so he explored his ideas through comedies full of clever quips and witty characters. His plays are "comedies of ideas" and he wrote them until he died at age ninety-five. Shaw is considered the only British playwright to rival Shakespeare in the last 300 years. Like Ibsen, Shaw was considered subversive at first. His plays were regarded as unfit for public discussion. Victorians called Shaw a "shocking disbeliever" and churchmen called him a "heretic." When Shaw's plays were finally introduced in the United States, they were withdrawn from libraries or prohibited by police from being staged. His plays survived the criticism, however, and are often produced today.

## THE ABBEY THEATRE IN IRELAND

The independent theater movement had an impact in Ireland, too. Up to the twentieth century Irish playwrights wrote in English for English audiences. They weren't encouraged in Ireland where there was so much poverty, a powerful Church and few theaters. Soon Irish writers turned to the Irish stage when William Butler Yeats, Lady Augusta Gregory, and the independent tea heiress Miss Annie Horniman (who once crossed the Alps from Italy to Munich, Germany alone) founded the Abbey Theatre in Dublin, Ireland. It would become the national theater of Ireland. Yeats, Gregory, and Horniman wanted to preserve Irish culture, and they encouraged writers to pen dramas on Irish themes, with Irish scenes and Irish people.

Lady Augusta Gregory was a middle-aged widow with no writing experience. Suddenly she began writing short, popular folk comedies based on the lives of the peasants she knew well. William Butler Yeats wrote poetic dramas in verse that were based on Irish myths and legends. As a theater manager Yeats was willing to run any play he thought was worthy for a couple of weeks even if no one came. For most of his working life Yeats was the guiding spirit of the Abbey Theatre, holding it together

*Scene from an Abbey Theatre production of* The Playboy of the Western World *by John Millington Synge, with Ger Ryan as Pegeen Mike and Barry Lynch as Christy Mahon. Courtesy Abbey Theatre, Dublin, Ireland.*

through many difficult times.

For a long while the playwrights and actors of the Abbey Theatre made their work a labor of love because the theater managers could not afford to pay salaries or royalties to the writers. However, since the Abbey Theatre was subsidized and the company had their own building, they didn't have to move from hall to hall to perform. The Abbey developed a company of professional actors who became known for their high standards and simple and honest acting. The Abbey's best and most important writer during its early years was John Millington Synge, who was sometimes called the "Irish Ibsen." Many of his plays are comedies based on the lives of Irish village folk. Synge's first play, *In the Shadow of the Glen*, describes an unhappily married Irish couple. Like most realistic drama during this period, Synge's drama *The Playboy of the Western World* was met with outrage. Every night groups came to the theater to prevent the play from being staged by jeering, shouting, blowing tin trumpets, or throwing raw potatoes. Seventy policemen were stationed in front of the theater and on nearby streets to keep the crowds under control.

In 1912 when this play toured the United States the actors were arrested briefly and charged with presenting a play that would corrupt public morals. In New York City audience members let off stink bombs during the show. Lady Augusta Gregory received an anonymous letter with the picture of a gun and a coffin on it that said her "doom was sealed."

In *The Playboy of the Western World* Christy Mahon is treated like a hero when he tells everyone that he killed his tyrannical father. When his father, who isn't dead, returns, the people turn on Christy and call him a criminal. This drama shows the joy, humor, bitterness, ugliness, and frustration of life in Ireland. Irish audiences saw it as a slander on Irish people. They didn't want to be "disturbed" by seeing a true view of Irish life because they were used to Irish life being pictured as happy and carefree. Synge, who was very sensitive and often ill, was shattered by this experience. It was the last play he lived to finish. When he died in 1909 no outstanding new plays were staged at the Abbey Theatre until 1923.

## THE MOSCOW ART THEATRE IN RUSSIA

Of all the new independent theater groups, the most important and influential on the theater of the Western world was the Moscow Art Theatre in Russia. Actor and director Konstantin Stanislavsky was dissatisfied with the state of acting and theatrical production in Russia. Professional actors were held in lower regard in Russia than in the rest of Europe. Many actors had been serfs—property of the nobility—who were trained as performers by being whipped and beaten. Other serfs were better trained and treated, but acting in Russia still was artificial and overdone. The Imperial theaters, which were controlled by the czars, had a monopoly on Russian drama. The playwrights were underpaid, foreign stars played the leading roles in plays—mainly melodramas and romantic plays—and the scenery was shabby.

### The Founding of the Moscow Art Theatre

Stanislavsky had first acted as a boy in a log cabin theater his parents built for him on their estate, and his imagination had been sparked further by the tours of the Meiningen Company from Germany. Vladimir Nemirovich Danchenko, a playwright and literary advisor, shared Stanislavsky's feelings. In 1897 during an eighteen-hour meeting in an artists' cafe they created the Moscow Art Theatre. Stanislavsky and Danchenko vowed to devote themselves to carefully rehearsed and detailed realistic productions of Russian and foreign plays.

### Anton Chekhov

The fourth play the Moscow Art Theatre staged was *The Seagull* by Anton Chekhov, who was a medical doctor, a playwright, and the grandson of a slave. Until he was nine, Chekhov was a serf whose father beat him and later deserted him. *The Seagull* was greeted with insults and jeers when it was first produced at the Alexandrinsky Theater. At that time Chekhov fled the theater in humiliation and later said, "Never will I write these plays or try to produce them, not if I live to be 700 years old." The problem as Chekhov saw it was that the actors of the old

*Scene from an Actors Theatre of Louisville production of* The Seagull *by Anton Chekhov with Ray Fry and Beth Dixon. Photograph by David Talbott. Courtesy Actors Theatre of Louisville.*

school couldn't act like ordinary people, like the characters in his plays.

Chekhov's dramas, which are neither comedies nor tragedies, are about people. The action in the plays is simple, with no surprising climaxes, great suspense, or confrontations. Instead, there is a sense of character, believable, touching human beings, and the complex relationships between them. Chekhov seems to be saying, "This is what life is like for this group of people." He was a careful observer of people and he captured them in his works, including *The Cherry Orchard, The Three Sisters*, and *Uncle Vanya*.

Chekhov wrote about the members of the decaying and helpless Russian aristocracy who could not cope with the changing times and longed for the way things were. Some of Chekhov's characters, decent people who feel lonely, useless, and unfulfilled, dream of improving their lives. Some rebel and reach out for what they want, most fail. But even while Chekhov shows us the trivial, boring aspects of life and shows characters who can't always say what they feel, he lets the laughter and bits of hope shine, too. Chekhov never lost his faith in mankind for whom he had great sympathy and understanding.

*A scene from* The Cherry Orchard *by Anton Chekhov, presented at the Civic Repertory Theatre, New York, 1928. Courtesy Drama Library, Yale University.*

## The Cherry Orchard

In Chekhov's most famous play, *The Cherry Orchard*, an aristocratic and once rich family is faced with the likelihood of losing their country home. They take no action to save the estate because they are unable to cope with their changed fortunes. In *The Cherry Orchard* not much seems to happen. The characters talk a lot but often get no response from anyone because they can't communicate with each other. Unlike plays of ages past, the characters' situations don't change—there are no rescues, no fortunes found to make someone rich, no happy ending. The play's picture is honest, true to life, and touching.

## A New Acting Style Needed

The performers at the Alexandrinsky Theater didn't know how to play the roles in *The Seagull* because the characters were unlike any they had acted. Chekhov's characters use pauses, broken sentences, stifled exclamations. Sometimes they say one thing and mean something else. Other times they mean much more than they say. Their dialogue is like that of real life. It wanders, abruptly changes to another subject. Deep feelings are expressed through subtle gestures, glances, or tones of voice.

Vladimir Danchenko convinced Chekhov to let the Moscow Art Theatre stage *The Seagull*. Because the characters in Chekhov's plays are individual, complex human beings, not stereotypes, the actors and directors had to discover a style of performing that would present Chekhov's characters as truthfully as possible. Stanislavsky trained his actors to do this. As a result, *The Seagull* was a success this time. Chekhov, Stanislavsky, and the Moscow Art Theatre continued to collaborate, and the seagull became the symbol for the Moscow Art Theatre. Today Chekhov's dramas are playing somewhere in the world at all times.

## Imagine Yourself the Actor

If you became an actor in Stanislavsky's ensemble, you would see how his rehearsals differed from rehearsals you had been involved with in the past. You would know why his performers could bring truth and realism to a production where actors of the "old school" could not.

Rehearsals are held in a barn from eleven a.m. to five p.m. and then from eight p.m. to eleven p.m. At the first rehearsal you find yourself not on stage but sitting around a table with the other actors. First, the play is discussed. You need to have a basic idea of the play. You exchange ideas on how the various parts should be played, and Stanislavsky makes sure that you understand the character you will play. Each line is analyzed for its underlying meaning. How different from other theaters you worked for in the past where rehearsals were so brief! You only knew your own part and you never read the entire play.

You know that you won't stand on stage until the play is read and understood because Stanislavsky doesn't want his performers just to say their lines and use gestures and other movements in a mechan-

*Konstantin Stanislavsky as Gaev in the 1904 Moscow Art Theatre production of Anton Chekhov's* The Cherry Orchard. *Courtesy of The Billy Rose Theatre Collection, The New York Public Library for the Performing Arts, Astor, Lenox and Tilden Foundations.*

*A scene from* The Three Sisters *by Anton Chekhov, presented at the Ethel Barrymore Theatre, 1942. Courtesy Drama Library, Yale University.*

ical way or according to some well-known code. You won't be allowed any longer to play a death scene by clasping your chest and tearing the collar off your shirt.

Stanislavsky wants you and the others to believe everything you do on stage. You must do what you believe your character could or might do. You've heard that some famous actors in the company take up to a year of study and rehearsal to perfect one role. *Hamlet* was rehearsed for two years before it was staged. Before interpreting the role of Colonel Vershinin in Chekhov's *The Three Sisters*, for weeks Stanislavsky wore the military uniform he would wear on stage.

## Production Design Under Stanislavsky

As director, Stanislavsky needs time to give careful attention to other details of each production, too. Like the Meiningen Company, Stanislavsky wants a unified production, each aspect contributing to one total effect. He will only recreate the atmosphere of a work after either visiting the location of the drama's action or after extensive research. Each play has its own setting to fit its theme and mood.

To recreate sixteenth century Moscow for the play *Tzar Fyodov Ivanovitch*, the theater company visited fairs, monasteries, and shops inside Russia and purchased objects from the sixteenth century, including cloth, furniture, cups, dresses, and wooden plates. Genuine robes and jewels of the period were borrowed from museums. Costumes were either original from the times or exact copies based on historical documents and made from the old materials.

Stanislavsky felt no detail was insignificant. He created a total world on stage that included common sights and sounds. The Moscow Art Theatre was noted for its sound effects. Onstage you could hear plates, forks, and knives clattering, windows shutting. You could hear leaves rustling, insects buzzing, or dogs barking offstage. If you saw the Moscow Art Theatre's production of *The Three Sisters* you would know that spring was approaching because you could see buds on the treetops. In the second act you would know it is winter because outside the house you would see the roofs covered in snow and hear the stove humming.

## The New Style of Acting

In these real settings how could an actor recreate the behavior of a real person? A character would no longer be a type, but a complete person. The actor couldn't rely on chance or inspiration or just playing himself. He couldn't just represent an emotion like love or anger by standing or looking a certain way. He needed to feel the emotion and then find a way to show it externally.

Stanislavsky knew that actors needed techniques and exercises to help them. For over thirty years he thought about the art of acting, the problems that actors face. He experimented and tested his ideas for training actors. He never stopped reevaluating his discoveries, correcting and changing his methods to adapt to new times, plays, and actors. Stanislavsky's principles would help performers build their characters, no matter what roles they played, by tapping their own creative powers.

Stanislavsky's theories and practices about training actors and helping them develop roles were spread throughout the world by his disciples and through his books, including *My Life in Art* and *An Actor Prepares*. The actor's body and voice need to be thoroughly trained to respond to any demands. Actors need to observe human behavior. They must find an inner justification for what they do on stage.

One way to do this, Stanislavsky stated, was through the use of "the magic if." "If I were this person faced with this situation, what would I do?"

Another useful concept that Stanislavsky developed was that of "emotion memory." The actor takes a dramatic situation that he must play but which is unfamiliar to him; despair at the loss of his wife, for example. He relates it to a similar emotional situation from his own life. The actor recalls the way he felt in real life when his character faces the comparable situation on stage. This allows him to feel the right emotion in his role. Finally, each time an actor plays a role he has to pay attention to the other actors and respond to them. He won't get stale in his part. It will be as if everything is happening for the first time.

## Tolstoy and Gorky

Stanislavsky's books have instructed generations of actors and represent the most comprehensive study of acting ever done. The Moscow Art Theatre has been and is one of the major theaters of the world. In Stanislavsky's own time, two other outstanding playwrights' works were produced at the Moscow Art Theatre. The first, Leo Tolstoy, is best remembered for *The Power of Darkness*, a grim tragedy about Russian peasants. Performance of it was forbidden in Russia for several years because it implied that the upper classes had their wealth at the expense of the poor who lived in squalor. When it was staged peasants were brought into the theater as consultants on the manners and customs of their people.

The other playwright the Moscow Art Theatre introduced was Maxim Gorky, "Maxim the Bitter." Gorky was a champion of oppressed people and he struggled to offer them a better life. He understood their plight because he was orphaned at the age of seven, bullied by his grandfather, and put out to work at age nine. When he was a teenager, Gorky ran away from his employer and joined a caravan of tramps and pilgrims. Gorky educated himself and soon was engaged in revolutionary activities, fighting the czarist government, and suffering police persecutions and imprisonment. Even in his prison cell he wrote about the potential worth of man and his hatred of the system that kept so many people in misery and poverty.

Gorky's most famous play is *The Lower Depths* which, like most of the realistic plays we've been introduced to, is still staged today. If you watched this play at the Moscow Art Theatre you would see a setting that depicted a cellar below Moscow somewhere. There you would see the outcasts of society—the Baron, a young thief, an actor, a streetwalker, a bitter old philosopher, and a dying woman. A pilgrim named Louka appears and listens to their dreams of goodness. Under Louka's influence they begin to change and fill with hope. Unfortunately, the landlord is accidentally killed by the young thief and Louka disappears. Without him most of the characters sink back into hopelessness. You leave the theater feeling pity for the characters.

To show this "slice of life" Stanislavsky took the actors to the infamous Khitrov Market where a community of tramps and thieves lived in underground passages. The actors drank with these people and listened to their personal secrets. On stage for the play the actors wore real rags and dirty shoes. The setting included dirt and soot on the floor and used mattresses. The picture of these people and their world was so realistic that audiences didn't want to sit in the front rows of the auditorium. They were afraid of getting lice.

Such realism in playwriting, acting, and production was born in the late nineteenth century. Realism made it possible to expand what the theater could do. It brought excitement, energy, and life back to the theater. Realism has become the major type of theater in the Western world, but not everyone was satisfied with realism. Even Stanislavsky, Ibsen, and Strindberg felt stifled working in the realistic style. They would do more experimenting and so would many others.

## THE INDEPENDENT THEATERS

Independent theaters still existed. These theaters made it possible for the new realistic plays and production styles to be seen. Other independent theaters would appear. They would have different names, like the Neue Freie Volksbühn in Germany and the Royal Court Theatre in London, but all would welcome and explore new writing, acting, and production styles that couldn't get staged elsewhere. Many of these independent theaters, also known as art theaters, little theaters, and experimental theaters, gave a small number of performances and had poor, unstable existences, but they defended artistic values. The independent theaters offered an alternative to the established commercial and state-run theaters.

# 6. MODERN THEATER DEVELOPS: REVOLTS AGAINST REALISM

The journey through theater history from the eighteenth century to the late nineteenth century was like a march toward realism on stage. But no sooner were there productions in the realistic and naturalistic styles than many people revolted against realism. Some said that realism in the theater was too narrow a view of the world. They argued that realism only shows what we can see in the world around us. "What about people's emotional states, feelings, and dreams?" they asked. "How do we show that part of man's experience on stage?" Others argued that realism ignores the mysterious and poetic parts of life. Another group was annoyed with the realistic theater's emphasis on putting every detail of a scene on stage, and they wanted to simplify the stage setting. Playwrights, designers, and directors, who often had nothing more in common than a dislike for realism, wrote and staged plays that tried to show reality and human experience in different ways.

## SYMBOLISM

The first revolt against realism was symbolism, which developed in France during the 1880s. The symbolists felt that the realists purposely showed the worst parts of life. Instead, the symbolists selected subjects from the past, fairy tales, fanciful stories, or fables. Many of these were love stories. The symbolists felt that true reality isn't what we sense in the world around us. It can only be found in the mysterious unknowable forces, feelings, and states of mind that control people's lives. These truths about life can't be stated directly through everyday dialogue, action, and scenery. Instead, they need to be hinted at and suggested through poetic language and symbols that can convey concepts and feelings.

In symbolic plays, scenery, movement, and speech are purposely unrealistic. Actors use unnatural gestures, they move slowly and speak in a sing-song as if their voices are coming back like echoes from a distant world. The actors might perform in near darkness or recite their lines behind a veil so they are like shadows or figments of the imagination. Odd and unrealistic costumes add an eerie quality to the characters. The settings are simple, with little furniture or props, sometimes made only of light and color on a backdrop. Often a gauze curtain was hung just behind the proscenium arch so the action seemed to be taking place in a timeless void.

### Lugné-Poë

Imagine yourself at the performance of a symbolic play at the Théâtre de l'Oeuvre in France. Here symbolist works are produced under the leadership of Aurélian-François Lugné-Poë, an actor who is willing to produce any experimental or original play. Only an independent theater would stage the symbolist plays since the established theaters found these plays incomprehensible. Lugné-Poë staged many of the plays of the first major symbolist playwright, the Belgian Maurice Maeterlinck.

### Maurice Maeterlinck

This evening you are watching a play by Maeterlinck, *Pelléas and Mélisande*, a love story with a sad ending. Like many of Maeterlinck's plays, the setting is an old castle hidden in the dark interior of a forest. The two backdrops are painted in swirls of greens, blues, and grays to suggest the castle, the forest, and the gloomy, misty atmosphere. The characters move and speak as if they are in a dream. It seems as though some hidden force determines what they do.

*Pelléas and Mélisande*, like most of Maeterlinck's plays, is short so this evening you also see his play *The Blind*. In the middle of an eerie forest you watch twelve blind men and women who sit in a circle. They are waiting for the priest who will guide them to safety. It's difficult to see anything in the bluish semidarkness in which the play takes place. Not much happens, the characters don't move, and what the characters say in soft, unexpressive voices doesn't seem important. However, the situation and the mood that Maeterlinck create make you wonder about the deeper meaning of every word and action you see and hear. At the end of the play you are puzzled. These plays are so different from anything you have seen.

Maeterlinck felt that plays need to suggest what the inner life of man is like, not the ordinary physical life we see. He also wanted to suggest the truths of life and the invisible powers of the universe. In his plays, which also include *The Intruder* and *The Blue Bird*, he tried to suggest and hint at meanings. In one play a rose might appear again and again until you wonder if it's just a rose. Maybe it's a rose that symbolizes beauty, love, or innocence.

Symbolist plays are usually vague and not easy to understand. They were difficult to stage. Many were too long or the action was too undramatic. However, the work of the symbolists at Lugné-Poë's Théâtre de l'Oeuvre influenced other playwrights like Ibsen who used elements of symbolism in their realistic works. Lugné-Poë's productions with simplified settings and costumes had an impact on stage directors, including Stanislavsky who was sometimes dissatisfied with all the realistic detail on stage.

## SELECTIVE REALISM

Many individuals would use selective realism on stage. They would select just enough props and scenery to put on stage to suggest the setting. An oversized bed with an enormous canopy was used in one production to suggest a king's bedroom. A huge canvas across half the stage represented a painter's studio in another play. Theater artists would also use objects as symbols.

## ROMANTICISM

Other writers rebelled against realism in the theater. Edmond Rostand wrote several fine romantic plays, including *Les Romanesques*, which is the basis for the

*A scene from an Oregon Shakespeare Festival production of* Cyrano de Bergerac *by Edmond Rostand. Henry Woronicz as Cyrano de Bergerac, Michelle Morain as Roxanne, and Marco Barricelli as Baron Christian de Neuvillette. Photograph by Christopher Briscoe. Courtesy Oregon Shakespeare Festival.*

popular American musical *The Fantasticks*. In Rostand's most famous play, *Cyrano de Bergerac*, Cyrano is in love with Roxanne, but he doesn't tell her so. He feels she can never love him because of his extraordinarily large nose. The young handsome soldier Christian also loves Roxanne, but he is so awkward with words that he finds it difficult to express himself to her. The eloquent Cyrano feeds Christian the words, so Christian becomes the handsome expression of Cyrano's feelings. *Cyrano de Bergerac* was retold in the 1987 movie *Roxanne*, starring Steve Martin, and it is often staged in amateur and professional productions, especially in the United States.

## FANTASY

James M. Barrie of England also rebelled against realism and wrote several fantasies. In his most famous play, *Peter Pan*, the young boy Peter Pan escapes far from the real world. Instead of growing up and facing adult responsibilities and problems, Peter befriends Indians, frolics with mermaids, and battles pirates. James Barrie insisted that only women play the role of Peter. In the United States Mary Martin played Peter on Broadway and in the classic television production. Recently, gymnast Cathy Rigby has flown across the stage as Peter. James Barrie loved children, and he stipulated in his will that all the royalties—money collected from selling the book version or from staging *Peter Pan*—should be given to the Great Ormond Street Children's Hospital in London, England.

## STRINDBERG'S DREAM PLAYS

Barrie took audiences to fantasy worlds, and Maurice Maeterlinck took them to unnamed worlds that seemed to exist out of time and place. August Strindberg, who had written realistic plays, now took audiences on a voyage into the unconscious mind of an individual. Strindberg was influenced by the psychologist Sigmund Freud, who stated that a person's unconscious mind—the part that he's not aware of—has power over his behavior. Freud said that the irrational things people do are caused by unconscious desires in a person's mind. He emphasized that people's dreams give clues to what is going on in that secret part of the mind.

Strindberg wrote a series of plays in the forms of dreams to show people's states of mind, to show how they perceive the world. In *A Dream Play* and *The Ghost Sonata* Strindberg tried to show the disconnected pictures in the mind of someone who is dreaming. There is no logical sequence to the actions, the events are unconnected and irrational, the time and place change often, and the characters dissolve or transform into others. One short scene follows another. The world appears to look like a nightmare, disordered. As Strindberg said of *A Dream Play*, "Anything may happen, everything is possible and probable. . . ." In one scene a castle grows and burns, and a huge chrysanthemum bud on the roof of the castle flowers, while human faces, full of misery, float through the air. Strindberg made little money in his lifetime. His dream plays were criticized in his native Sweden, and often he was on the verge of insanity. His dream plays, however, had a great impact on modern drama. With them Strindberg created a new form of playwriting in which images and symbols were used to show what was going on in someone's mind.

*A scene from* A Dream Play *by August Strindberg. Courtesy Swedish Information Service.*

*A set by Adolphe Appia for the opera* Parsifal, *Act I: The Sacred Forest. Courtesy Drama Library, Yale University.*

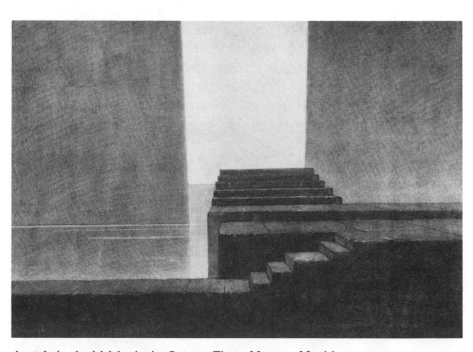

*A set design by Adolphe Appia. Courtesy TheaterMuseum, Munich.*

# REVOLUTION IN SCENE DESIGN AND LIGHTING

During this period of upheaval and questions in the theater, two men set a foundation for a revolution in the visual aspects of the theater—scenic design and lighting. Their ideas helped make it possible to stage the new symbolist dramas and other new dramas that would follow. One of them was the Swiss Adolphe Appia, who never attended the theater until he was nineteen and who as an adult lived like a hermit in a castle. The other was the Englishman Edward Gordon Craig, son of the actress Ellen Terry, who appeared on stage at the Lyceum Theatre from the age of eight.

## Adolphe Appia

Adolphe Appia advocated putting three-dimensional, solid settings on stage to complement the actors' three-dimensional bodies. He felt that steps, ramps, and platforms would give the actors a more useful playing space than flat painted scenery. Appia's set designs are simple because Appia felt that nothing should detract from the movement of the actors. He also felt that designers only needed to suggest the setting. The spectator should use his imagination to complete the picture. A garden didn't have be shown in full detail; it was enough to have a garden wall, a few pots of flowers, and a tree.

Light, according to Appia, could unify all the elements of a play. Light could blend the scene and the actors. A simple set painted in neutral colors could be lit in such a way that the actor's shape and movement would be emphasized. Light, Appia theorized, should change depending on the mood, emotion, or action of a play. Lighting might change as time passed, or moment to moment, or the color and intensity of the lights could suggest shifting moods. For the opera *Siegfried* Appia said that there was no need to represent a forest but instead "the feeling of a man walking through a forest." He achieved his effect by playing light and shadows against the trunks of a few trees. To suggest a field Appia used a neutral background, a few fabric hangings, and beams of light that shone on the floor of the stage. Appia called this use of light "living light" and he regarded light as the "supreme scene painter."

## Edward Gordon Craig

Edward Gordon Craig was a dreamer who, because he ignored the actor and the limits of the theater, often infuriated people who worked in the theater. Craig didn't understand actors and said, "The actor is for me only an insuperable difficulty and an expense." He suggested replacing the actor with a "super-marionette" at one point. What he really wanted was an actor who could do anything the director asked of him and would obediently do as he was told. Craig's theories of stage design were brilliant but for the most part impractical, so few theaters asked him to design their productions. Instead he inspired others who carried out his ideas.

Craig advocated the use of huge, simple, abstract forms and shapes—levels, stairways, blocks, and cubes—on which the actors could perform and be arranged in different groupings. Craig also advocated huge, grand, tall screens placed at different angles

*A set design by Edward Gordon Craig. Courtesy Drama Library, Yale University.*

and in various combinations on stage. These mobile panels would turn, advance, recede, and move as needed to create the different places where the action took place. This combination of screens and abstract shapes, which would change color under different light, would suggest a particular environment. Craig felt this type of scenery freed the actor from what he saw as the clutter of realistic staging, which he hated. This scenery would say more by suggestion. "Let the theater be poetic and imaginative," Craig declared. Craig also felt that one main set piece should suggest a setting. For Shakespeare's *Macbeth*, instead of creating several elaborate settings, Craig designed a massive rock surrounded by mist.

For Ibsen's play *Rosmersholm*, Craig read the description in the play of the "large old-fashioned and comfortable living room," but he didn't recreate a living room in detail. Instead he interpreted another description of Rosmersholm as a "house of shadows." Craig designed a space with ordinary sacking painted in overlapping streaks of blue and green. He placed a huge barred window in the background and a few pieces of furniture on the stage.

In 1912 Craig designed a production of Shakespeare's *Hamlet* for the Moscow Art Theatre. For the first scene he filled the stage with towering screens that seemed full of mysterious corners, passages, and deep shadows. Craig planned that the huge screens would be moved as the scenes changed before the audience's eyes. One hour before the play was to begin on the first night, the whole arrangement of screens crashed to the floor. This was a perfect example of Craig's vision and impracticality.

Craig and Appia worked independently, but together they founded a new stagecraft. They both criticized the theater of their time and offered solutions. At first they were condemned as mad theorists, but later they were praised as prophets and saviors. They invented simplified stages with abstract shapes for the actors to move on and used light as an element of the total stage picture. Their sets suggested the environment or mood of a play with a few details. The realists would recreate a cathedral in every detail, while Craig and Appia might suggest the cathedral with a pillar, an arch, and a candelabra. Appia and Craig also envisioned a master artist or director who would coordinate every facet of a production—creating, directing, and interpreting the play. They inspired designers and directors in Europe and America.

### William Poel

In England William Poel used simplified stagings for Shakespeare's plays. At The Elizabethan Stage Society Poel designed a theater to approximate Shakespeare's stage. The audience surrounded a platform stage on three sides, and the background was a wall with two doors and a balcony. Audience members used their imaginations to turn the single setting into different places.

Simplifying the stage picture as Poel did was fairly easy, but many of Appia's and Craig's simplified designs required sophisticated machinery. During this period from 1875 to 1915 there were many innovations in technology that made the dreams of Appia and Craig possible. The revolving stage, an idea that came from the Japanese theater, allowed for fast and smooth scene changes. A huge circle was cut out of the stage floor and mounted on wheels so it could be turned. Different settings could be placed back to back, and each would appear to the audience in the opening of the proscenium arch in turn as the stage floor revolved. With the rolling platform stage, settings could be mounted on a large platform offstage and then moved onstage by rollers set in tracks. On an elevator stage, the stage was divided into segments, and each section could be set at a different level or the elevator could be used to raise heavy objects from beneath the stage.

## MAX REINHARDT: INDIVIDUALISM AND SPECTACLE

The innovations in theater technology and in nonrealistic and realistic theater introduced from 1875 through the early years of the twentieth century came together in the work of the German Max Reinhardt. Reinhardt left school when he was fourteen and worked for three years in a factory, then in a bank. Defying his parents, Reinhardt took acting lessons, and at eighteen he had his first professional acting job. He went on to become an internationally acclaimed director.

Before Reinhardt each theater was dedicated to one method of production. Reinhardt believed that each play required its own style of production, and the same play could be staged in different ways depending on the time and place. He mounted all types of plays, including Shakespearean, realist, and symbolist, and used acting and staging techniques from all periods of theater history, including those of Eastern cultures such as Japan. No one method, interpretation, or point of view was the right one according to Reinhardt. As Reinhardt said, "All depends on realizing the specific atmosphere of a play and on making the play live." The author's text and its faithful interpretation were most important to Reinhardt.

Reinhardt produced plays in a variety of theaters including a ballroom; on all sorts of stages, including proscenium arch and platform stages. He staged the Greek play *Oedipus Rex* in an empty circus arena, the Schumann Circus. Here there were no sets or decorations, just the ring, which was used for a large chorus as the Greeks had done two thousand years before. A wide staircase connected the ring to a platform surrounded by six huge columns. Behind the platform was a wall with a central door. There was no curtain or proscenium arch, and the audience sat on rising tiers of steps.

Shakespeare's *Twelfth Night* was staged in the Old Outdoor Riding School at the base of a sheer cliff in Salzburg, Austria. There the galleries and boxes for the spectators were carved from solid rock. Reinhardt used other outdoor locations around Europe for his productions. His greatest achievement of this type was an annual festival in Salzburg. Reinhardt used the whole city for his production of the medieval play *Everyman*, in which a man is summoned by Death. The production began in daylight at Cathedral Square on a wooden platform with no scenery or properties. The cathedral served as a backdrop.

When Everyman was summoned, voices called from all sides of the town and the sound echoed from the towers of the many churches in Salzburg. When Everyman's soul was lifted to heaven, the inside of the cathedral lit up, the massive gates opened, and organ music swelled from inside. All the bells of the city's churches began to peal. By this time night had fallen, and the only light came from the brilliantly lit marble and gold interior of the great cathedral.

Reinhardt also staged large, spectacular shows for huge audiences in cathedrals and in amphitheaters. For *The Miracle*, which was his most grandiose and costly spectacle, Reinhardt took the Olympia Exhibition Hall in London and converted it into a gothic cathedral. The hall was reconstructed to hold tall

*Max Reinhardt's production of Sophocles'* Oedipus Rex, *St. Petersburg, 1912. Max Reinhardt Archive, Special Collections, Glenn G. Bartle Library, State University of New York at Binghamton.*

columns and tiers of steps on three sides for the audience. An enormous stained glass window was designed to illuminate the thousands of performers in this drama. Reinhardt hoped to make the audience participate in the religious experience of the play.

Reinhardt also used smaller theaters for intimate productions. He staged plays in The Kammerspiele, or The Chamber Playhouse, which had only three steps and no orchestra separating the stage and the audience. Here plays such as those of Ibsen and Strindberg could be staged.

Not only did Reinhardt search for the right space in which to stage each play, he also tried to create the right relationship between the actors and the audience. For the play *Sumurun* he used a runway in the Japanese style that extended from the stage far into the audience. Reinhardt also dreamed of a "Theatre of the Five Thousand," a gigantic theater that would hold as many people as the Greek and medieval theaters had. Here the audience would have a sense of surrounding the action and sharing in a communal experience, as the Greek and medieval audiences had done. In 1919 Reinhardt opened the "Grosses Schauspielhaus," which seated 3,300. The horseshoe-shaped seating surrounded an arena behind which was a raised proscenium stage.

Reinhardt was one of the best loved directors of his day. Even though he paid actors little money, they wanted to work with him. Unlike Edward Gordon Craig, who regarded actors as a nuisance, Reinhardt listened to the actors' ideas about the production and he encouraged and developed the talent of many performers.

Max Reinhardt popularized many of the new ideas, plays, and staging practices that were slow to be accepted. He was one of the first to produce the expressionist dramas that would emerge at the end of World War I. Reinhardt used all the elements that could be used to create a stage production. He wasn't afraid to make the theater frankly theatrical—an art all its own, not necessarily an exact replica of real life. His theater was a complex of authors, actors, designers, and musicians depending on him to select and coordinate everything.

## THE DAWNING OF THE ERA OF THE DIRECTOR

Reinhardt became the first modern director to gain an international reputation. With Reinhardt, *director* became a word in the theatrical vocabulary. A director, as defined by Reinhardt, controls and unifies every aspect of a production. The director creates the performance by imposing a point of view on the play. The director has the vision and makes the choices. Other people like Saxe-Meiningen and Stanislavsky directed, but they also had other jobs in the theater, for example, as actors. Reinhardt directed.

The twentieth century in the theater is the era of the director in the way the eighteenth century was the era of the actor. In the twentieth century society no longer held a common outlook on the world. People weren't coming to the theater, as the Greeks or Elizabethans had, with a sense of shared experience. There was no world of total unity the theater could reflect. Directors had to create a new set of values and viewpoints each time they staged a production. Each director asked himself how he would accomplish this. There were many answers.

The theater no longer developed along one line from one style to another as it had in earlier centuries. There would be many experiments, many styles of writing, acting, and producing; many styles of design in costumes, scenery, and lighting, as well as in the stages and playhouses themselves. Many movements and experiments would fizzle. Some features of other experiments would influence later theater artists or be incorporated into contemporary drama. Through all these experiments the art theaters, the little theaters, would be there to welcome the new plays and production styles.

# 7. THE ERA OF ISMS: THEATER THROUGH THE 1930s

Expressionism, Dadaism, Surrealism, Constructivism—all these were movements in the theater from the 1910s through the 1930s. As we hopscotch from country to country, from the land of one "ism" to another, we'll see how some playwrights, scenic designers, and directors experimented to find ways to reveal more about people and their world than the surface realism of André Antoine and Konstantin Stanislavsky did.

## EXPRESSIONISM

Expressionism developed in Germany around 1910 and reached its peak in 1917 and 1918. Expressionist playwrights, including Georg Kaiser and Ernst Toller, were disillusioned by and revolted against a world in which there were so many powers that threatened people, like social injustice and capitalism. These playwrights protested against the technological developments and industrial revolution that they felt dehumanized people. They believed that people who worked in factories were becoming slaves to the machines or turning into machines themselves. They also saw man becoming trapped into seeking materialistic things.

In Ernst Toller's play *Transfiguration* a factory is equated with a prison. In Czech playwright Karel Čapek's *R.U.R.* (Rossum's Universal Robots), which became world famous, audiences saw how people who worked on assembly lines became more and more mechanical themselves. Čapek pictured a future in which all the workers would be robots, mechanical characters with no souls. It is Čapek who first coined the word "robot," meaning a mechanical drudge.

Expressionist playwrights also were horrified by a world that could produce a world war, World War I. They felt that the human spirit and man's soul were being destroyed on this planet.

Kaiser, Toller, and other expressionist playwrights felt that a new world was possible only through the regeneration of each person. Every

*Scene from a 1922 New York production of Karel Čapek's R.U.R. Courtesy of The Billy Rose Theatre Collection, The New York Public Library for the Performing Arts, Astor, Lenox and Tilden Foundations.*

human being would have to struggle against the de-humanized world of machines, military weaponry, and false values like materialism. Each person must base his life on humanitarian principles and must strive to create a world free of war and hate. In Ernst Toller's *Masses and Man* an upper class woman, Sonia, deserts her husband and leads the masses in a strike for peace. She wants to avoid mob violence and bloodshed, but another character calls for animal action. There is violence, which destroys the peace for which the masses had revolted. In the end Sonia is imprisoned and sentenced to death.

The expressionist dramas often revolve around an idea. The playwright has a message to convey, often a plea to reform man and society or to warn of some impending doom that faces the world. The plays often center on a lonely main character who rebels against the world to find personal fulfillment, to search for some deeper truth, or to look for a way to change the world.

This central character is often gripped by fear, anger, or some other violent emotion as he faces the strange world alone. He is often unhappy and tortured. Since the characters in these plays are symbols that often stand for an idea or represent many people, they are not fully developed, but character types. The main character is like an everyman surrounded by other characters who represent forces working against him. Their names reflect their occupation or family relationship. In Kaiser's play *Gas*, which shows modern civilization being destroyed by money-motivated industrialism, the characters include the Engineer, the Girl, the Gentleman in White, and the Billionaire's Son. In Toller's *Masses and the Man* the Nameless One stands for the mob spirit that will use violence to achieve its goal.

## Expressionist Production Style

The expressionist playwrights wanted to force the audience to experience the character's mental state. They wanted the audience to see reality, events, and the world through the central character's distorted inner vision. It was a challenge for scenic designers and directors to create the inside of a character's mind on stage, to depict a mad, nightmarish, disor-dered, chaotic world, to show events as the character sees them—strange, distorted, illogical. The stage pictures they created were often weird.

In these plays the scenes are short, shifting rapidly, in a frenzied way. They are not necessarily in chronological order, and act as a constantly dissolving picture. Settings might be fragmented and incomplete, on a mostly bare stage. A room could be suggested by a few pieces of furniture, a window, a door frame, and a few pictures hanging in mid-air. A birch tree bathed in blue light might represent a garden. Objects are often used symbolically, so death, for example, was sometimes represented by a snow-covered tree. Black and dark blue curtains were used as a background to suggest a void where characters and set pieces appear and disappear like magic. Scenery, shapes, and colors were exaggerated and distorted. Even furniture and props were enlarged to suggest moods of violence or bitterness. Buildings or the walls of rooms tilted or leaned in as if to threaten the main character. The sky might be green rather than blue to reflect a character's jealous feelings.

In *From Morn to Midnight* by Georg Kaiser, a tree changes into a skeleton and beckons the main character. This famous play is about a bank clerk whose attempts to free himself from the meaninglessness of modern society lead to his suicide. This clerk sees the world as unreal so the play makes the world look unreal. In one eerie and lonely scene the clerk spreads out his arms and looks as if he is nailed to the cross as Jesus Christ was. Audiences interpreted this visual symbol to mean that the end was near for the clerk.

## Lighting

In expressionist plays light was used to create a mood or an atmosphere. Often there were several scenes set up on the stage at the same time, and light was used to focus on the scene where the action was taking place at a given moment. Sometimes light was used to behave like the mind. It would drown in darkness what it wanted to forget and cover in light what it wanted to remember. Light could be used in other symbolic ways, too. It would grow dim when a character died, for example.

## Unrealistic Acting Style

The settings and the lighting in these productions were unrealistic and so was the acting. The actors often wore mask-like makeup that made them look pale, with darkened eye sockets. This made the characters look anguished and tortured. Actors moved mechanically, abruptly, spasmodically, and with extreme energy. They used a variety of exaggerated movements and gestures. An actor would reach for an object not just with his hands, but with his whole body. If an actress were expressing anger she would tense her body, bare her teeth, and show bulging eyes. An actor would show despair with bowed head, eyes hooded and body collapsed. The actors' dialogue was described as "telegraphic," or abbreviated, short, clipped and jerky, often with sentences that are only one or two words long. The lines were delivered in a breathless, tense, quick manner.

## Leopold Jessner

Leopold Jessner was the major director in the expressionistic style. He liked to use enormous flights of steps and platforms to suggest the world of the play and to give the actors different levels on which to perform. Jessner used steps the way Craig envisioned using screens and curtains. He also used simplified scenery—one or two set pieces to suggest the scene. In addition, he used bold primary colors, bright lights, and symbols that were very obvious.

In Jessner's production of *Richard III* by William Shakespeare, Fritz Kortner, who played the dangerous tyrant Richard, wore different colored clothing to symbolize Richard's status at different points in the play. He began the play in a black costume in front of a black curtain to symbolize evil. At the end of the play when Richard is defeated, the actor wore white clothing and a white curtain dropped down behind him to signify that virtue had triumphed. Finally, when Richard dies the actor was covered by a bright red spotlight to indicate blood and death.

Jessner used steps symbolically, too. For his production of *Napoleon*, Jessner placed the actor playing the title role at the top of a flight of steps, and he placed the officers below to show the relationship between Napoleon and the officers. At the end of the play when Napoleon the emperor is defeated, audiences saw him seated on the lowest step with the sinking sun behind him and the soldiers seated above.

## DADAISM

The expressionist theater created many powerful, collage-like visual images. Another movement developed at about the same time as expressionism. Many young theater artists, especially from Germany and France, fled to Zurich, Switzerland during World War I. There, under the leadership of the Romanian Tristan Tzara, they created *Dadaism* or *Dada*. These theater people were disillusioned and bitter. To them the world made no sense; it had to be meaningless and insane to produce a world war. So their theater was senseless and meaningless, too.

Dada was spontaneous and illogical, often made up of anything that popped into the creator's mind. Even the name Dada, which means hobby horse, was chosen randomly. It was the first name that Tzara and his friends found in their French dictionary. These artists didn't present plays, but "programs," which were chaotic, with several things happening at once. In one program a person pounded on a drum, a performer in a clothes wardrobe insulted spectators, and a voice called from under a hat in the shape of a sugar loaf. Another program consisted of lectures, a reading, dances, visual art, and short plays. This theater was bizarre. Its artists wanted to shock audiences, to destroy traditional values, but they didn't attempt to create anything new to replace what they were eliminating.

## SURREALISM

The Dadaists didn't last long but many of their ideas fed into another movement called *Surrealism*. The leader of the surrealists, André Breton of France, stated that playwrights should write "automatically." He, like others, wanted to get at a deeper reality than what we see around us. Surrealism means "beyond realism." Breton said that these deeper truths are found in the unconscious mind. To set these thoughts free, writers were supposed to let their ideas pour out spontaneously. The results often seemed like nonsense but were supposed to be more profound than just recording what is seen around us.

Guillaume Apollinaire's play *The Breasts of Tiresias* is an example of a surrealistic play. Apollinaire's theme in this play is that if a nation wants to prosper it needs a large population, so women must have many children. He suggested that as women are liberated they have fewer children and the population declines. The main character Therese becomes a man. She even gives up her breasts, which are represented by balloons that she explodes. Her husband now must have the children and he bears 40,049 babies. Other characters in the play are like lunatics. One character represents the entire population of Zanzibar. Speeches are shouted through a megaphone. Apollinaire rejected everyday logic and shocked audiences in this play, which was performed only once, at a private performance, during Apollinaire's lifetime. In addition to playwriting, it's believed that Apollinaire was an art thief.

## THE AVANT GARDE IN FRANCE

### Alfred Jarry

Dada and surrealism are considered part of the *avant-garde*, the experimental in French theater. They were inspired by the dwarfish, bowlegged young playwright Alfred Jarry and the 1896 production by Lugné-Poë of Jarry's play *Ubu Roi* (*King Ubu*). When Jarry's play was staged it was unlike anything else at the time, it was so unrealistic, and many in the audience hated what they saw. Like other worthwhile, "ground-breaking" plays that had appeared on the French stage in the past, it was greeted at its two performances by audiences who whistled, hooted, threw things, and rioted.

*King Ubu* began as a schoolboy prank; Jarry wrote the first version when he was fifteen. The character of King Ubu is a caricature based on Jarry's high school physics instructor. Ubu is gross, fat, and amoral. He swears and waves a toilet brush as a scepter. He's a cowardly, pompous assassin who murders a young Polish king and takes over the throne. Much of the plot centers on the battles

fought between Ubu's armies and those of the rightful heir to the throne.

Jarry wanted to show the audience all of its negative qualities—greed, cruelty, stupidity, selfishness, and vulgarity. He wanted to shock people, confront them with this play on the theme of power and the aggressiveness and violence that go with it. Jarry also purposely created a play that would go against everything an audience expected to see on stage.

When *King Ubu* was first staged, the scenery was painted to represent outdoors and indoors at the same time. At the back of the stage the audience saw apple trees in bloom under a blue sky. Against the sky was a small closed window and a fireplace through which the characters entered and exited the stage. A bed was painted on the left side of the stage and at the foot of the bed there was a bare tree with snow falling. There were palm trees on the right side

*Artist's intepretation of Father Ubu in* King Ubu *by Alfred Jarry. Illustration by Claudia Mullaney.*

of the stage and, there, too, a door opened against the sky. A skeleton dangled beside the door.

The audience was outraged, but they went into an even greater uproar when an actor stood on stage, held out his left arm, and the actor playing King Ubu put a key in the other actor's hand as if he were putting a key into a lock. The actor swung his arm as if it were a door opening and made the noise of a bolt turning. André Antoine was in the audience and at this point he started a demonstration against what he felt was Jarry's thumbing his nose at stage realism.

It might seem amazing that a play written by an author when he was a teenager would have such an influence on the theater in decades to come, but Jarry turned traditional forms of playwriting and staging upside down. His work was violent and aggressive. There was no recognizable reality. The action was unpredictable, and the language was crude. Jarry was mocking people, shocking them. Many of these and other elements he used would be used by future theater artists, including having someone place posters on a hook stating where each scene was taking place, and unrealistic props like cardboard horses slung around the actors' necks to suggest they were horses.

Alfred Jarry died at a young age from opium abuse and frequent periods of malnutrition. There were many times in his life when he had little to eat. When there was lots of food Jarry started at the end of the meal. He ate dessert first and ended his meal with a bowl of broth.

## Jacques Copeau

Many of the ideas of the Dadaists, surrealists, and of Alfred Jarry would influence theater artists in the years ahead but they were only a small part of the experimental theater in Paris, France during this period. The person with the most immediate and greatest impact on French theater at this time was Jacques Copeau. Director, actor, and teacher, he disliked the realistic theater and wanted to get rid of the machinery and showy effects and instead use simplified settings. For example, in one play Copeau simply hung an electric light bulb in a tree to show a suburban area.

Copeau envisioned a playhouse and a theater stripped to only what was essential so attention could be focused on the actor. To Copeau the actor was the only necessary element of the production. Copeau believed that the director should analyze the text of each play he presented very carefully and then train his actors to deliver the meaning of the play on stage using their bodies in an expressive way. The play's text alone — without special staging effects — would stimulate the imaginations of the audience and the performers. The theater Copeau visualized would also break down the barrier between the audience and the performers. There would be no obvious division between them. No longer would the proscenium arch divide them.

Jacques Copeau realized his dreams beginning in 1913 when he took over a theater in Paris, renamed it the Théâtre du Vieux Colombier, and simplified the fancy, ornately decorated playhouse and auditorium so that it looked stark, almost like a hall in a monastery. Over the next decade he altered the playing area until it evolved into what has been labeled the first "presentational playhouse" in the modern world. The Vieux Colombier had no footlights or proscenium arch, no line marking the stage from the auditorium. The actors could have more direct contact with the audience. The stage was bare — no wings, no painted backdrop. It did have a permanent setting: a balcony against the back wall with an arched opening in the middle. This single background could be altered with screens and a few pieces of furniture or properties to stage any play. Most of the light came from four large lamps hung in the auditorium.

At the Vieux Colombier, Copeau staged all types of plays from medieval to classical, from poetic to contemporary. He produced plays by unknown playwrights and unknown works by known playwrights. Copeau paid as much attention to his actors' techniques as he did to the type of stage on which his players should perform. In 1924 he took his company of young actors to Burgundy in the French countryside. There Copeau established a school where his students underwent intensive training. Copeau stressed that his actors be physically and technically trained. He wanted his students to feel free to use

*The stage of the Vieux Colombier, Paris. Phot. Bibliothéque Nationale, Paris.*

mime, dance, improvisation, and acrobatics as means of expressing themselves on stage.

## EXPERIMENTATION IN RUSSIA

Much theatrical experimentation occurred in Russia after the Russian Revolution of 1917. The czars who had ruled for centuries were forced out of power by the working class who were hungry, weary, and miserable from World War I. Now the Communists ruled the country, and they wanted to break with the past and create new theatrical forms. From 1918 to 1924 there were hundreds of new theatrical ventures, including dramatic groups in factories and villages and the creation of children's theater. The government provided financial and material support for these experiments. There was excitement and adventure as theater artists tried to create a new dramatic style for the audience in this new society.

### Vsevolod Meyerhold

The most daring and innovative experiments were conducted by Vsevolod Meyerhold. He began his career with the Moscow Art Theatre but soon revolted against realistic staging techniques. He wanted to bring back a sense of wonder to the theater and to make the theater "theatrical" — an art in and of itself, not necessarily a reflection of real life. He always wanted the audience to be aware they were in the theater.

Meyerhold wanted to blend elements from film, radio, circus, music hall, comedy, and sport into a spectacular show that would reflect the new age of technological wonders. He believed this new form would become the art of the new society. To create this new form, which would be fast-paced, flexible, and full of humor, joy, and surprise, Meyerhold used all the modern technology available. He borrowed from other theatrical styles like the commedia dell'arte and the Kabuki theater of Japan. He also used symbols and stripped the stage to its barest essentials. Meyerhold wanted to break down the barriers between the audience and the stage so he built gangways and steps from the stage into the audience and had his actors move in the aisles.

### Constructivism in Settings

Meyerhold frequently filled his sparse stage with an abstract set, consisting of a combination of some of the following: stairs, ladders, ramps, turning wheels, suspended platforms, springboards, scaffolding, and trapezes. For *The First Distiller* Meyerhold created a set of suspended and mobile platforms, flying trapezes, and poles. Nothing was hidden; all the bolts and struts and metal machine parts were visible so the set often looked like a bridge construction. This style of setting was not decorative, but functional. It was considered a "machine for acting" because the actors could move over, around, and on the set or swing from it. This style of setting was called *constructivism*.

## The Biomechanics of Acting

Meyerhold did not use realistic sets as Stanislavsky did, and he didn't have his actors base their roles on psychological motivations the way Stanislavsky did, either. Instead, Meyerhold invented a method of training his actors called *biomechanics*. He wanted to develop actors who would be part athletes, part acrobats, and part animated machines. They were trained in gymnastics, circus movement, and ballet to be flexible and in control of their bodies. They were skilled in juggling and mime, too. The performers learned how to control every movement and gesture to express emotions because to Meyerhold emotions and ideas were expressed best through physical activity. For example, a performer could convey the feeling of joy by swinging on a trapeze, turning a somersault, or going down a slide.

If you attended Meyerhold's production of *The Magnificent Cuckold* in 1922 you would see his ideas brought to life. The stage is stripped bare, not even a curtain, with just the brick wall of the stage showing. In the center of the space are scaffolding and slides. There are several platforms connected by staircases and gangways. You also see wheels, rolling discs, a trapeze, and windmill sails. The lighting is bare and bright. The actors, wearing no makeup and dressed in light blue overalls like mechanics, run, jump, and swing on the set.

## State-Controlled Theater

While Meyerhold is now recognized as one of the most important directors of his time, in the 1930s his voice was silenced. By 1936 the state controlled all the theaters in Russia. Government officials ruled that "socialist realism" was the only acceptable material for Russian plays. Dramas had to be written in the realistic style and staged the same way. They had to convey a political message and glorify the

*Artist's interpretation of the set for Vsevolod Meyerhold's production of* The Magnificent Cuckold. *Illustration by Michael Sitarz.*

Soviet government. Even the works of dead playwrights had to conform to Soviet teachings to be produced. The government wanted to use the theater to educate the masses in the beliefs of Communism. They wanted to put an end to experiments and anything abstract like symbolism because they felt the worker audience wouldn't understand it.

Beginning in the 1930s, 80,000 members of the Communist Party served as censors in the theater. Each new play had to be approved by a special agency and anything that didn't conform to "socialist realism" was condemned. Meyerhold's productions were criticized, and he was called "politically dangerous." In January 1938 his theater was closed and Meyerhold was left unemployed and isolated. The Communist Party tried to win him over, and in June 1939 he was given the chance to denounce everything he stood for at a convention of theater directors. Instead, Meyerhold defended his point of view. Josef Stalin's secret police arrested him as a German spy, and he disappeared into an Arctic concentration camp where he was tortured and, many believe, murdered.

Many writers and theater artists were arrested, sent to concentration camps, or executed by firing squads. The era of Russian theater experimentation was over. Beginning with Josef Stalin's regime from 1930 to 1953 and continuing to the mid-1980s, there was theater everywhere in Russia, theater that continued to be an important tool to educate and indoctrinate people in the ideology of Communism.

# NEW PLAYWRIGHTS

## Luigi Pirandello

Many of the revolts against realism in the theater in the early decades of the twentieth century were in the way plays were staged, but some of the rebellions were in the way plays were written. One playwright who blasted the realistic style, which pretended that the theater was an imitation of real life, was the Italian Luigi Pirandello. He doubted whether the theater could reflect reality because he didn't think we can observe reality. Pirandello said that it is hopeless for people to recognize reality because

reality and truth are always changing. Truth and reality are different from person to person; they change depending on the circumstances.

Pirandello's personal life led to his asking, "What is real? What is truth?" His life was an unhappy one. His father arranged his marriage to a girl Pirandello had never met before, and she eventually went insane. Pirandello took care of her at home for fifteen years and only his writing provided him some consolation. Through his wife's illness he came to see that reality is what an individual thinks or perceives it to be. If you think the world is pink and fuzzy and full of cuddly bears that is your reality. The way I see reality may be entirely different. Who can say which is the right, the true reality?

Pirandello stated that all values are relative and that we can never be sure of anything, especially about other people. How can we know the truth about other people when people wear "masks" to hide their true selves. You can pretend to be sophisticated, and I may not discover that you are really insecure. So the truth could be the opposite of what I believe.

Pirandello presented his ideas on stage in many challenging and original plays. His themes and techniques were radical enough that audiences were baffled and perplexed. Pirandello's plays are full of unusual complications. They end with questions left unanswered. Critics found him dangerous, and toward the end of his life most theaters refused to stage his plays. In 1934, however, Pirandello received the Nobel Prize and today Italians regard him as their greatest playwright.

Pirandello's best known work is *Six Characters in Search of an Author*, which was first produced in Italy in 1921. In it Pirandello explores the idea that the stage is a world, too. He examines how the real world and the stage, which is supposed to be an illusion of the real world, relate to each other. In this work, six characters from a play invade the stage during the rehearsal of another play by Pirandello and tell the director that they want him to stage their lives instead because their author didn't finish their story. As these characters demonstrate what it would involve to tell their story, they live their story. Confused? So were audiences. Here were actors

*A 1936 production of Luigi Pirandello's* Six Characters in Search of an Author. *Courtesy of The Billy Rose Theatre Collection, The New York Public Library for the Performing Arts, Astor, Lenox and Tilden Foundations.*

pretending to be actors rehearsing a play. There were actors playing the part of the "characters" who invade the stage, and there were actors playing the parts of actors playing the "characters." Most audiences gave up trying to figure this out. Here was a "play-within-a-play," but what was the real play and what represented real life?

## Federico García Lorca

The work of two other playwrights from the continent of Europe stands out from the 1920s and 1930s. The writers were the Spaniard Federico García Lorca and the Frenchman Jean Giraudoux. In spite of the brutally repressive country in which García Lorca lived, he managed to write many fine plays with imaginative language. He wanted to bring beauty into drama and to show that the world was full of passion and poetry. García Lorca showed how

people suffered because they were full of passions that clashed with the strict social customs and codes they were expected to live by. Not only did he write about feelings in conflict with customs or reason, but he wrote about the battles between love and honor, life and death. García Lorca wrote with great emotion about the tragedy of life, but also about the love of life and his belief that love is what makes people truly alive. His three most famous plays are tragedies exploring these themes: *Blood Wedding*, *Yerma*, and *The House of Bernarda Alba*.

García Lorca's life was cut short when he was caught up in the turmoil of the Spanish Civil War. Although he was not political, he was executed by a firing squad when he was only thirty-eight. Francisco Franco's forces won the war and under his Fascist regime the Spanish theater faced severe censorship. At least García Lorca had the opportunity to give Spain its best plays since the Golden Age of the sixteenth century.

## Jean Giraudoux

Jean Giraudoux was a former teacher who began writing plays when he was in his forties. He wanted to introduce a serious drama that would also appeal to audiences who went to the commercial theaters. The director Louis Jouvet collaborated with Giraudoux and introduced his plays to the public. Like García Lorca, Giraudoux treated the theme of opposing forces in his plays—peace and war, life and death, freedom and duty. His characters must decide between two contradictory positions.

Giraudoux took most of his plots from well-known myths and legends. Even though his plays were serious, he wrote with imagination and humor. His characters ranged from gods and water sprites

*Louis Jouvet in a scene from* Amphityron 38 *by Jean Giraudoux. Courtesy French Cultural Services.*

to peasants and derelicts. In *Amphityron 38* he explored the nature of love. Many of his other plays were protests against war and greed. In *The Madwoman of Chaillot*, produced in 1945 after Giraudoux's death, he introduced audiences to a charming but eccentric madwoman who lures the world's bankers and businessmen into the sewers of Paris where they disappear forever. The play is fun and fantastic, but very serious, too. Giraudoux used this clever fantasy to show his hatred for materialism.

## ENTERTAINING THEATER IN ENGLAND

While playwrights, actors, scenic designers, and directors in Germany, France, and Russia experimented in the theater, theater people in England worked in traditional ways. In England, the theater wasn't shocking, it didn't provoke people or challenge them, but theater that entertained was as popular as ever. Several fine directors and many excellent performers developed, and one popular playwright stood out.

### Noel Coward

Noel Coward was an actor, a playwright, a composer, and a director who wrote for the commercial theater and enjoyed great success. He left school at an early age, appeared on stage when he was eleven, and wrote his first play when he was eighteen. Coward went on to write many plays and musical comedies, but he is remembered most for his entertaining, sophisticated comedies that showed the behavior and manners of the upper classes, especially the conflicts in their love lives. Like English playwrights before him, Coward wrote in a witty way. The audiences who saw their lives on stage laughed instead of getting offended. Among his plays are *Hay Fever, Cavalcade*, and *Private Lives*, the latter still popular. *Blithe Spirit*, which is the story of a man who is remarried but haunted by the meddlesome ghost of his first wife, is still staged, often in high school productions.

### The Old Vic

One theater stands out in England during the 1920s and 1930s. The Old Vic was a worn, degraded the-

*A scene from the Asolo Theatre Company's 1989-90 production of* Blithe Spirit *by Noel Coward, with Kimberly King, Pat Nesbit, Joseph Culliton, Jane Strauss, and Susan Willis. Photograph by Alan Ulmer. Courtesy Asolo Center for the Performing Arts.*

*Laurence Olivier as Romeo, Edith Evans as Nurse, and John Gielgud as Mercutio in* Romeo and Juliet. *Courtesy of the Board of Trustees of the Victoria and Albert Museum.*

ater, which under the management of Lilian Baylis and then Tyrone Guthrie became the most loved theater in London and was devoted to producing Shakespeare's plays simply. The Old Vic was a training ground for young performers. They were underpaid and overworked, the conditions weren't great, all the actresses shared one sink, but they were given wonderful opportunities to play the big roles in Shakespeare's plays and other classics.

## Outstanding Actors

Many outstanding performers developed at the Old Vic and it came to be called the "cradle of stars." These stars included Peggy Ashcroft, Sybil Thorndike, Edith Evans, Ralph Richardson, John Gielgud, and Laurence Olivier. Many of them continued in starring roles for many decades. Sybil Thorndike never went more than two months without being in a play from the time she was four. Ashcroft thought of becoming a professional actress when she was fourteen, but was told that she would never be an actress. She began performing at age eighteen and later was labeled one of the "classiest" actresses in England.

Ralph Richardson came from a family of Quakers who disliked anything to do with the theater. When he was a young actor, a director told him he was "awful." Edith Evans was unattractive and shy, but she had a talent for creating characters so managers always gave her leading roles. Evans said that even though she was plain, she could suggest the qualities of a pretty woman because she went onstage believing that she was beautiful.

## Laurence Olivier

All of these performers were excellent. Some branched out from classical and Shakespearean roles, others starred in films as well as on stage. One actor, however, stands out from the rest—Laurence Olivier. When he was seven Olivier thought it was fun to make an audience believe he was somebody else and he soon decided, "I'm going to be a simply smashing actor." One of his first acting jobs was with a troupe called the Lena Ashwell Players, which toured different theaters. Often they played to audiences in swimming baths, or large indoor pools. Oliv-

ier and the other performers often had to dress in the bathrooms, called lavatories in England, and they came to be known as the Lavatory Players.

As a young actor Olivier had a terrible problem that lost him one acting job: he couldn't stop giggling on stage. He overcame his giggling and went on to work in several fine theaters including the Old Vic. There he developed his acting abilities and portrayed the great Shakespearean characters, including King Lear, Hamlet, Richard III, and Othello. Olivier performed on stage and in films for over fifty years and was praised for his combination of natural instincts and control of his technical skills, voice, and body.

## IRISH THEATER

### Sean O'Casey

The Irish theater wasn't experimenting much either, but one outstanding playwright developed during this period. Sean O'Casey was the Abbey Theatre's first outstanding writer since John Millington Synge. O'Casey wrote about the struggles of the poor working-class people who lived in the city slums of Dublin, Ireland where he grew up. O'Casey's journey from poverty to playwright was a long and difficult one.

O'Casey was the last of thirteen children. He lived in a crowded, smelly apartment, had little to wear, and barely survived on hard bread and tea. Because of his poor eyesight, he left school at an early age and was illiterate until he was fourteen. Slowly and painfully he taught himself to read and write, often going hungry so he could use what little money he had to buy books. He earned his money in a variety of jobs, from working fifteen hours a day as a newsboy to breaking stones on the roads. For fifteen years he worked and wrote plays which the Abbey Theatre rejected. He had no money for paper and ink so friends gave him paper from the offices where they worked and boxes of indelible lead pencils. O'Casey boiled the purple lead pencils in water so he could make ink to write his plays.

O'Casey was over forty years old when the Abbey Theatre produced his first play, *The Shadow of a Gunman*, and later such plays as *The Plough and*

*A scene from Alabama Shakespeare Festival's production of* The Plough and the Stars, *with Neal Moran, Eddie Rutkowski, and Jack Parrish. Courtesy of the Alabama Shakespeare Festival.*

*A scene from Alabama Shakespeare Festival's production of* The Plough and the Stars, *with Mimi Earnest and Becky Watson. Courtesy of the Alabama Shakespeare Festival.*

*A scene from Alabama Shakespeare Festival's production of* The Plough and the Stars, *with David Weincek and Terry Wells. Courtesy of the Alabama Shakespeare Festival.*

*A scene from an Arena Stage presentation of* Juno and the Paycock *by Sean O'Casey, with Denis Arndt and Tana Hicken. Photograph by Joan Arcus. Courtesy of Arena Stage.*

*the Stars*, and his masterpiece, *Juno and the Paycock*. In these plays and others set in the Irish city slums, O'Casey painted an honest picture of the strengths and weaknesses of these humble people he loved. He set their stories against the background of historic events in Ireland, the uprisings and struggles for an Ireland independent of England.

In his plays O'Casey depicted Irish men who talk about fighting for their beliefs, but who don't take action, and the Irish women who quietly, but with strength and self-sacrifice, keep their families and their country alive. In *Juno and the Paycock* audiences watched Juno maintain hope and struggle to go on as her family falls apart. Her husband hates to work but likes to drink, her daughter is rejected by a boyfriend, her son is killed by a rival political group. O'Casey's plays could be depressing, but he shows people's courage, he shows moments of humor, and he tells his stories in beautiful, poetic language. His subjects speak for all time because they are universal — love and hate, joy and despair, life and death.

## EXCITING TIMES FOR THEATER IN EUROPE

The years between World War I and World War II were exciting and rich for the theater in Europe. Playwrights like Sean O'Casey and Noel Coward, Federico García Lorca and Jean Giraudoux maintained a high standard of writing, while actors and actresses in England set a high standard of performance. The expressionists, who were influenced by August Strindberg and Luigi Pirandello, explored new forms of playwriting while the constructivists pushed the theater into new ways of using the stage and the performers. Jacques Copeau envisioned a different playhouse and playing space.

All these people influenced future generations of theater artists, but two individuals from this period had a great impact on theater in the twentieth century. Antonin Artaud inspired others through his theories, and Bertolt Brecht showed a new purpose for the theater through his plays and his stage productions.

# 8. ARTAUD AND BRECHT:
# THEATER OF CRUELTY AND EPIC THEATER

Antonin Artaud of France and Bertolt Brecht of Germany were deeply affected by the overwhelming problems that confronted people in their time. Both men believed that the theater could help humanity solve its problems, but their ideas of how the theater could help change society were very different. Brecht's Epic Theater was a political theater, while Artaud envisioned a magical theater, a ceremony or ritual, which he called a Theater of Cruelty.

## ARTAUD'S THEATER OF CRUELTY

Stage and film actor Antonin Artaud was dissatisfied with most European theater because it only dealt with the psychological problems of individuals or the social problems of groups. Artaud wanted a theater so powerful that it would get at the subconscious mind of each individual. It would be a cruel theater because it would make spectators uncomfortable,

forcing them to confront themselves, whether they wanted to or not. Spectators would face all their destructive and primitive instincts like anger and hate. These performances would show people that they have the potential to be mean, brutal, and violent.

Artaud stated that these feelings, which people keep inside, are the cause of a person's problems within himself and with other people. But the "theater of cruelty" could release these forces. It could heal a sick world by cleansing people, removing the feelings that divide men and result in social injustices and war. Artaud's theater would also release positive forces and show the good potential of humans. The "theater of cruelty" would lead to the salvation of mankind.

The existing theater in Europe couldn't accomplish what Artaud envisioned. In fact, Artaud never fully realized his ideas, but he never stopped writing about them. On the subway, in restaurants, and in

*Antonin Artaud in* The Passion of Joan of Arc, *a 1928 film. Courtesy of The Museum of Modern Art/Film Stills Archives.*

bed, sitting or while leaning a notebook against a wall, Artaud wrote down his theories. He was first inspired by a troupe of Balinese dancers who performed in Paris. Artaud sat in awe as one dancer entered a trance, became possessed by the dance, and through it expressed something about the world beyond that we see. From this the dancer seemed to gain an indefinable command over the audience. Artaud started to see the power that a ritualistic performance in the theater could have.

## Reaching People's Senses

Instead of a theater with dramas that concentrate on telling a story or presenting characters, Artaud's theater consisted of rituals and ceremonies. It didn't rely on a play-text or words. Instead, his theater was more like a primitive experience, more felt than understood. His theater attacked people's senses, surrounding them with a combination of sounds, gestures, dance, lights, music, movements, and colors all at the same time.

Artaud felt that words couldn't communicate so he searched for a new language based on signs and gestures. The performers used their voices for cries, groans, chants and to create effects. For example, all the actors might hum in a whisper that builds to a roar.

## The Theatrical Space

To get a gut level, involuntary response from people, Artaud wanted the actors to surround and approach the audience on all sides. He got rid of the proscenium arch. Instead there was a large common space with no division or barriers between the spectators and the actors. Performances took place in garages, airplane hangars, abandoned factories, barns, and warehouses. The audience was seated in the middle of the space, and the actors performed around and in the midst of the audience, in the corners, along the walls, and overhead on catwalks that ran all the way around the playing space.

Artaud staged few productions, most of which were failures, and he had only one published play, *Jet of Blood*. For most of his working life he was addicted to drugs, which he took for an illness and as part of his search for a magical theater. He spent many of his final years in an insane asylum.

## Artaud's Effect on Other Playwrights and Directors

Artaud also dedicated decades of his life to the theater. His theories, which he presented in the book *The Theatre and its Double* in 1938, were not accepted immediately, but almost twenty years later they captured the imagination of playwrights and directors. Jerzy Grotowski in Poland, Peter Brook in England, Roger Blin, Ariane Mnouchkine, and Jean Genet in France were inspired and challenged by Artaud's new concept of the theater.

## BERTOLT BRECHT

Bertolt Brecht, playwright, poet, and director, built on the ideas of another German, the director Erwin Piscator. Piscator and Brecht worked in Berlin, the capital of Germany's new Weimar Republic. It was an exciting city for theater artists in the 1920s. Max Reinhardt and Leopold Jessner were experimenting there, and plays were being staged in forty different theaters. Berlin, like the rest of Germany, also had many problems caused by their defeat in World War I. There were strikes, food riots, hunger, poverty, and unemployment.

## The Influence of Erwin Piscator

Piscator shared the expressionists' desire to transform society, but he thought their methods were too vague. Piscator created a political theater and staged plays that explored current issues. He wanted to appeal to working-class audiences, to get them to see their problems and those of their country on stage and to do something about their condition in real life. To get his audiences to make connections between what they saw on stage and what was happening in the world, to move them to reform society, Piscator used every type of technology available, including machinery and movies.

In 1927 when Piscator staged *Hurrah, We Live!* by Ernst Toller, he created a set consisting of metallic scaffolding divided into different playing areas. This set represented the many classes of people in society. Often different scenes took place in the various playing areas at the same time. In other scenes the actors performed in one area while a film was shown in another space to comment on the action on stage, to suggest that what happens on stage is a reflection of what is happening in life.

Piscator's 1927 production of *Rasputin* by Alexei Tolstoy was staged in a huge revolving steel circle, which symbolized the earth. Film clips were shown on the outside of the globe and words were projected on side screens, again to make people think about what they were seeing.

Piscator used film and projections, slides, animated cartoons, charts, and maps to document what audiences saw on stage, to put what they saw on stage in a larger social and political context. In 1920 for the play *The Hour of Russia*, Piscator used a large map for the set, which showed the geographical location of the action and described the political meaning of the scenes.

## BRECHT'S EPIC THEATER

*Epic theater* is the term that came to describe this type of theater. Bertolt Brecht perfected the style and made it his own. Brecht felt that the world could be changed for the better, and he saw the theater as the tool to bring about these changes. The theater could entertain, but it also must serve as a lecture platform, a place to teach, change people's attitudes, and encourage them to improve society. As Brecht said, his purpose was "to teach us how to survive." Brecht first came to these conclusions during World War I when he cared for the wounded in a German army hospital.

Brecht wrote plays that show how social forces make people act the way they do. He explored the problems of good and evil, justice and injustice. He showed how a capitalist system is evil because it squashes the poor and makes rich people corrupt. In *The Good Woman of Sezuan* he showed how impossible it is to stay good in a capitalist society. Brecht also portrayed the evils of industrialization, the military, and war. In an early play, *Drums in the Night*, and later in the play *Mother Courage and Her Children*, Brecht showed people who make money from war.

Brecht knew that it would not be easy to get audiences to think about what they were seeing, to judge it objectively and then to go out, act on what they saw, and bring about changes in society. He invented a new type of playwriting, staging, and acting to create a thinking audience.

## Theater Outside the Emotional Experience

Brecht didn't want audiences just emotionally involved in what they saw. Instead, he always wanted to remind them that they were in a theater watching a play that reflected a problem or an attitude that exists outside the theater in the real world. To accomplish this he invented the *Verfremdungseffekt*, "strange-making effect" or "distancing effect." Brecht found ways to jar the audience, interrupt them from their emotional involvement with the characters, to make things strange enough so they would ask questions about it, evaluate it. If they *felt* too much they wouldn't *think* enough. Brecht used many devices to achieve this distancing effect. Some he invented, some were developed by others.

Instead of writing plays that build to a climax, Brecht wrote plays that consist of episodes — separate situations that could each stand alone, separate incidents or events that deal with the same general subject. The scenes were separated by songs, dance, film, speeches, pantomime, slides, and signs. Each of these elements made its own comment on the action. This was one way to jar audiences and to interrupt their emotional involvement with the play. There were many others.

## Staging *The Threepenny Opera*

Imagine that it is 1928 and you are watching what will become Brecht's most famous musical, *The Threepenny Opera*. In it you see characters, from all classes, who are trying to get whatever material goods and money they can. You see how their greed causes misery. At the rear of the stage are two large screens. At the front of the stage there is a white half curtain on a steel wire. You can see all the preparations for each scene behind the half curtain. On the screens a written outline is projected of the events in each scene. Because you know what is going to happen you're not held in suspense so you think about

*A scene from Great Lakes Theater Festival's 1989 production of* The Threepenny Opera *by Bertolt Brecht and Kurt Weill, with William Leach and Carol Morley; directed by Victoria Bussert at the Ohio Theater, Playhouse Square Center. Photograph by Roger Mastroianni. Courtesy Great Lakes Theater Festival.*

*A scene from the Sacramento Theatre Company's production of* The Good Person of Setzuan *by Bertolt Brecht. English version by Ralph Manheim. Mathew Davis as Yang Suhn and Terri McMahon as Shen Teh. Photograph by J. Kenneth Wagner. Courtesy Sacramento Theatre Company.*

*A scene from* Mother Courage and Her Children *by Bertolt Brecht. Courtesy German Information Center/Owen Franken-GIC.*

*A scene from The Guthrie Theater's 1965 production of* The Caucasian Chalk Circle *by Bertolt Brecht, with Helen Harrelson as the Governor's wife, Matt Talberg as Young Michael, Zoe Caldwell as Grusha, and Ed Flanders as Azdak. Courtesy The Guthrie Theater.*

the events more.

The titles and words of the songs are also projected on the screens while they are sung. A small orchestra is visible on stage throughout the play. Songs keep interrupting the play. A love song has biting, cynical words, but the music is sweet and pretty. In another serious scene the music is very lighthearted. This contrast between the music and the words makes you more aware of what the song and the dialogue are trying to say.

## Other Techniques of Brecht

The white half curtain that revealed what was happening on stage and the screen projections were two of Brecht's favorite distancing devices, but Brecht used many others, such as masks. In *The Good Woman of Sezuan* audiences meet Shen-Te, a kind-hearted prostitute who is given money by several gods, and Shui-ta, Shen-Te's male cousin whom she goes to for advice as more and more people try to corrupt her. The same actress plays both roles by wearing masks. Soon it becomes clear that Shen-Te and Shui-Ta are really two parts of the same person—the good and evil parts. As the play progresses Shen-Te becomes Shui-Ta for longer periods of time. Brecht used this device to show how in a materialistic, capitalistic society, a person has a choice to be good or bad. At the end of the play the gods tell Shen-Te to be good but they don't tell her how. The audience is supposed to leave the theater and solve this problem as it exists in the real world.

In *Mother Courage and Her Children*, a play about a mother who must choose between the well-being of her children and making money from the war, Brecht used a chorus, as the Greeks had 2000 years before. He had the characters step out of the scene to introduce themselves and talk directly to the audience. He used a revolving stage to show Mother Courage's wanderings, and he used large posters to introduce the action.

In *The Caucasian Chalk Circle* Brecht used the German version of a Chinese story. Often he used old stories and reworked them to make the audience feel that they were getting a report of past events, another way to distance them from the action. In *The Caucasian Chalk Circle* an infant prince is abandoned by his self-centered mother, and a young peasant woman rescues him and cares for him. When the real mother returns to claim the child so she can snatch the fortune he will inherit, the adoptive mother doesn't want to give him up because she loves him. A test is set up to determine who should keep the child. The child is put into the center of a chalk circle and each mother is instructed to grab an arm and pull. But beyond this story is the larger question of who should have a claim to things, to wealth, in the world. In staging this play Brecht used a singer to introduce and comment on each scene. This singer summed up the lesson Brecht felt the play should teach the audience.

Brecht never let audiences forget they were in a theater because he always called attention to the lighting, sets, effects, and machinery. In his productions, the stage lights were always visible and they cast a cold and bright light. The settings were not realistic. Only a few set pieces were used to emphasize the meaning of each play. When Brecht needed a moon he dangled it down on a piece of string. Objects entered the stage from above on visible ropes. Captions, maps, and other images were projected on screens.

## Brecht's Actors

If you attended a production of one of Brecht's plays you would find that you don't identify with the characters in the play, but you understand what they represent. You have this feeling because Brecht didn't train his actors to live their parts the way Stanislavsky's actors did. Instead, Brecht trained his players to understand a role, to interpret it, and to comment on it. These players narrated the actions of their characters. It was as though they had witnessed the events they were relating sometime in the past and were now reconstructing what happened and showing the audience what the action meant. They showed the reactions, gestures, and movements of these people, but they didn't become the people. It was like being an eyewitness at a traffic accident and then telling someone about it later. You could show how the victim reacted, but you didn't become the victim. Here was another way to distance audiences emotionally from what was happening on stage.

Brecht's actors worked very hard to achieve these effects. They rehearsed each play for many months. Brecht would test several ways to stage each scene. He didn't come to rehearsals knowing exactly how he wanted everything done. If Brecht didn't like the way something was working out, he would start all over again. He would scribble new lines and scenes and demand that his performers learn them immediately. Often, an actor would have his part changed overnight. On the day that Brecht's play *Baal* premiered, Brecht was calmly writing new parts of the play for that evening's opening performance.

## German Opposition

Bertolt Brecht's career spanned several decades and his interest in the theater began at an early age. He was nine years old when he ordered his brother Walter and the neighborhood youngsters to assemble their toy soldiers to act out a play. At sixteen he set up and directed a puppet theater at a friend's house. In the 1920s Brecht staged several plays in Germany. But in 1933 when the Nazis and Adolf Hitler came to power it became impossible for Brecht to stay in Germany. Brecht was opposed to this new regime and he spoke out against it. His plays were banned and Brecht was placed on an "elimination list." Many prominent playwrights, actors, and producers were killed. A few years later in Moscow under Stalin, Brecht's closest friends, theater artists, were murdered or imprisoned by Stalin's secret police.

Brecht was forced to leave Germany in 1933 with his wife, Helene Weigel, and their two small children. From 1933 to 1947 they lived in exile, fleeing from one country to another: Russia, Austria, France, Denmark, Sweden, Finland, England, Switzerland, and the United States. Little of Brecht's work was published or staged during this time. Yet during this unhappy, difficult time Brecht wrote his most important plays, *The Caucasian Chalk Circle*, *Mother Courage and Her Children*, *Galileo*, and *The Good Woman of Sezuan*.

Beginning in 1949 Brecht had the chance to produce his many plays. With major help from his wife, Brecht formed the Berliner Ensemble Theatre in

*Helene Weigel as Mother Courage. Courtesy KaiDib Films International, Glendale, California.*

East Berlin, which came to be recognized as one of the greatest theaters in the world.

It was Weigel who got an office building and had a rehearsal stage constructed in it. She located and rented apartments, found furniture, scrounged food, and attended to everyone's travel documents. Weigel was a remarkable woman for other reasons, too. When she was young, she gave up a brilliant theatrical career in the state-supported theaters to perform in her husband's small political productions. Weigel was a small woman, but people declared that on stage she seemed like a giant. She was a great German actress and was best remembered for her portrayal of Mother Courage. When Bertolt Brecht died in 1956 Helene Weigel ran the Berliner Ensemble.

### Brecht's Far-Reaching Influence

Like other innovators Brecht was called both a savior who had come to save the theater and a "wrecker" who was trying to "throw the German theater into a cesspool." Whatever people said, Brecht's ideas changed theater artists' concepts of playwriting, acting, and directing. Many theater artists came to use his methods of staging after World War II. He especially influenced playwrights in the German-speaking world, such as Peter Weiss. Brecht's plays, his staging, and his style still intrigue people.

## EFFECT OF WORLD WAR II ON EUROPEAN THEATER

The Nazis' rise to power, which saw Brecht and theater artists like Max Reinhardt and Erwin Piscator flee for their lives, ultimately led to World War II. The war used all of Europe as its arena. During World War II the theater was interrupted and slowed down, but it was not crushed completely. In France, even though there was always the threat of an air-raid alert and bombings, people attended the theaters. In Paris there were blackouts at night, no outdoor lights were left on, to make it more difficult for the enemy to hit targets, so people carried flashlights to find their way to the theaters. Often the electric power failed. Because there was a ban on heating in public places, audiences huddled to stay warm. Material was rationed during the war, but clever theater people found ingenious ways to create costumes. Paper was rationed too, but somehow posters and tickets were still made.

At the beginning of the war with Germany in 1939, London's forty-three theaters were closed for the first time since the Puritans shut them in 1642. It was difficult to get actors during the war because many of them were in the army, and often actresses played the male roles in plays. With a six p.m. curfew no one could be on the streets at night, yet some theaters managed to offer morning and afternoon performances.

# 9. THEATER AFTER WORLD WAR II: ABSURDISTS AND ANGRY YOUNG MEN

The world was left shaken and unstable by World War II. Adolf Hitler had ordered millions of Jewish people killed, the atomic bomb had destroyed the cities of Hiroshima and Nagasaki in Japan, thousands of soldiers and civilians across Europe had lost their lives in the fighting, dissidents had died in Russian concentration camps, and numerous cities had been leveled.

People reacted in many ways to these events. They were anxious, worried about the possibility of atomic war and the complete destruction of the earth. They felt uncertain and insecure and wondered if the human race could act responsibly or even survive. Other people felt alienated, separated, or cut off from society. Many individuals regarded themselves as objects manipulated by forces over which they had no control.

In the 1950s many dramatists were dissatisfied with the state of the world. They reacted in two main ways. One group wrote plays that showed everything people did as absurd and purposeless. The other group angrily put down the social and political conditions that they felt had created the problems.

## THEATER OF THE ABSURD

Theater of the Absurd developed in France in the 1950s. Several playwrights appeared about the same time. Although they worked independently and in different styles, they painted a similar view of life. They pictured a bleak world where there is no God, no purpose, no logic or order. They saw life as meaningless. They felt that it was futile for humanity to struggle and absurd for people to try to control their fate when the world had no certainty and seemed determined to destroy itself. These playwrights also showed people isolated from each other, lost and alone, humans who can't communicate with each other because language and words don't say anything.

### Plays of Dreams and Nightmares

Instead of telling a story with a beginning, a middle, and an end, these plays consist of situations that resemble dreams or nightmares to reflect the writer's view of the world. Sometimes scenes and actions are repeated or a play ends where it began. The characters engage in strange behavior and senseless, unexplained action. Their speech and dialogue are nonsensical to reflect their inability to communicate. If you view these plays as poetic images that paint a picture of a situation and not as realistic traditional plays, you will begin to understand them.

### Samuel Beckett and Eugene Ionesco

The most famous absurdist dramatists were the Irish-born Samuel Beckett and the Romanian Eugene Ionesco. Both worked in France and wrote plays in French. While their plays are staged worldwide today, like so many playwrights before and since who have presented something new and different, it took a long time for their plays to be accepted. Audiences were usually small and the critics were hostile because they couldn't understand the plays. Often the critics thought they were witnessing a hoax. Once again the small art theaters were there to welcome these plays as were a few directors with vision who believed these plays were worthwhile.

Samuel Beckett brought his manuscript of *Waiting for Godot* to five theater managers, but they either sent him away or didn't read the play. The actor and director Roger Blin, who would eventually direct all of Beckett's plays, wanted to present it but it took three years before he could get enough money to rent a small theater for one month, make posters, buy a roll of tickets, and pay each of the actors $15.00 a week.

Eugene Ionesco and his wife scraped together enough money for tickets, posters, and the actors' meals to be able to stage Ionesco's play *The Bald*

*Soprano*. The costumes were a gift. There wasn't enough money to pay the actors and, because there was no money to advertise, Ionesco and the cast wore sandwich boards and paraded up and down the sidewalks one hour before the first performance to get an audience.

Beckett's play *Waiting for Godot* is the most famous and probably the greatest absurdist drama. The play has been translated into over twenty languages and is still staged around the world. In it Beckett presented a visual image of the senselessness of life and the way people live isolated from others. The play is also about waiting — waiting for something or someone who will give meaning to our lives.

### Staging of *Waiting for Godot*

Imagine that it is 1953 and you are one of the thirty people in the audience watching the almost three-hour premiere of *Waiting for Godot* in Paris. You see a nearly empty stage with a backdrop consisting of odd pieces of fabric stitched together. A lone bare tree made of wire hangers covered with crepe paper stands on a foam-rubber base. Two tramps, Vladimir and Estragon, are waiting for Mr. Godot. They spend their time putting on their shoes, picking up their bags, taking off their hats, creating things to do while they wait for Godot.

Two strange men appear who seem to be a servant and master, but they soon leave. A boy appears and tells the tramps that Mr. Godot won't be coming today, but tomorrow. In the second act the tree has four leaves. It is supposed to be the next day, same time, same place. The two strangers return but one claims to be blind, the other dumb. Godot does not arrive and the tramps decide to go, but they don't move, nothing happens. You sense that they will go on waiting. This powerful image stays in your mind long after you have left the theater.

### *Endgame*

In 1957 you attend a performance of Beckett's play *Endgame*, which is set in a bare room with two small windows. Hamm, a blind, paralyzed old man, sits in a wheelchair. His servant, Clov, is unable to sit down. Hamm's legless parents, Nagg and Nell, are encased

in two garbage cans that stand by the wall. Only their heads stick out. These characters seem to be the victims and survivors of a nuclear holocaust. The world outside is dead and these people are searching for ways to pass the time while they live out their last days. But the end never seems to come. When you leave the theater you're confused, maybe irritated that you felt like laughing at what was a horrible situation. Often the absurdists infused humor into their tragic pictures.

### *Happy Days* and Other Plays

You are also fortunate enough in 1961 to see the outstanding French actress Madeleine Renaud as Winnie in *Happy Days* by Beckett. She would go on to play the role for twenty years. When the play begins you see Winnie, alone on stage, buried to her waist in a mound of earth, but she doesn't seem troubled by her situation. Every morning Winnie is awakened by a bell and she spends her time smiling and touching the objects in her purse. She follows this daily routine over and over again. She talks about the past and a few times she tries to talk to her husband, the only other character in the play.

In Act II Winnie is buried up to her neck and only her head is visible. You watch as she continues to talk, to ramble and repeat herself. Even though Winnie's situation suggests that she is alone and isolated and heading to her death (the mound is like a grave) Winnie talks and acts as though she's happy to be alive. The play ends and you are sure that Winnie will continue to hope and look for meaning in her life although death awaits her and she can't control anything. Again, you realize that what you have seen is a visual image of the futility of life in a senseless world as Beckett envisioned it.

Beckett continued to write plays and each involved *less* — less speech, movement, and setting, and fewer characters — to create his personal vision of life. In 1969 the production of Beckett's play *Breath* lasted for thirty seconds. It began with the cry of a newborn child and ended with the last gasp of a dying man. There was little to hear and nothing to see. In Beckett's *Not I* audiences saw only a chattering, disembodied mouth.

*A scene from a German production of* Endgame *by Samuel Beckett. Courtesy German Information Center/Owen Franken-GIC.*

*Portrait of Samuel Beckett. Courtesy Irish Tourist Board.*

## Ionesco's New Dramatic Forms

Eugene Ionesco, the other major absurdist, also created new play forms, dramatic techniques, and fresh images to explore his themes, yet Ionesco never intended to be a playwright. His first play came about when he was thirty-six years old and teaching himself English. He was intrigued by the phrases and practice sentences in a lesson manual and began playing with them. Ionesco started to realize what nonsense a lot of language is—it doesn't communicate anything. He expanded from there to create images that show the emptiness of middle-class life and, since Ionesco felt reality was nonsense, he created images to express this feeling of nonsense in his play. The result was *The Bald Soprano*.

In *The Bald Soprano* Mr. and Mrs. Smith talk in meaningless phrases as they go about their daily routine. They have a conversation about a large family in which all the members living and dead, male or female, whatever age, are called Bobby Watson. Another couple, Mr. and Mrs. Martin, enter and they talk to each other as if they don't know each other. They ask each other questions and learn that they live in the same house and are parents to the same child. Finally, they realize they must be married to each other. In this play you think you're hearing real conversations, but nothing makes sense.

The setting seems familiar but the action isn't logical. A clock strikes seventeen times and Mrs. Smith responds, "There, it's nine o'clock." The doorbell rings but no one is at the door. A fire chief arrives and he says he's in a hurry to put out fires, but he takes the time to relate a string of meaningless stories. The two couples then talk in phrases until their language breaks down into sounds. The play doesn't really end as the Martins replace the Smiths and repeat the same lines that opened the play.

Ionesco's play *The Chairs* was first staged in an old, unused hall that the actors paid for because none of the established theater managers in Paris would risk producing it. Imagine that you are watching the production with the other five people who have bought tickets. On this evening in 1952 you have no idea how successful this play will be in four years.

The play begins and you see two old people who, you learn, are expecting a crowd of dignitaries to visit them. They have invited these distinguished people to listen to the important message the old man feels he has to tell about the meaning of life. The old man and the old woman greet the guests and keep filling the stage with more and more chairs, but you don't see or hear anyone. The professional speaker arrives whom the old man has hired to deliver his message. Satisfied that the message will be given to these important guests the old man and the old woman jump into the sea. You watch as the speaker faces the crowd of chairs, and tries to speak, but he is deaf and mute and can only make gurgling noises. He tries to deliver the message by writing it on a blackboard, but it's only a jumble of meaningless letters. As you leave the theater you wonder what the play was about, especially the image of those empty chairs.

For Ionesco the chairs were important characters in the play. They represented nothingness, the emptiness of the world as Ionesco envisioned it. The entire play is like a poetic image of the inability to communicate, the meaningless of words, the futility of human life.

## Jean Genet

The Frenchman Jean Genet also wrote plays after World War II—bizarre, shocking plays. Like Samuel Beckett and Eugene Ionesco, Genet depicts characters who are lonely and isolated and can't find meaning in the world. Like Luigi Pirandello, Genet explores the conflict between how things appear and reality. The characters in his works play such a variety of roles to act out their dreams and fantasies that

there is no reality. Criminals pretend to be judges and bishops in his play *The Balcony*, for example. Genet also wrote about specific social and political issues of his time.

Genet's plays also are a product of his life. He was abandoned by his mother as an infant and placed in a foster home. When he was ten Genet's foster parents called him a thief and he decided to live up to the role. At fifteen he was sent to a reformatory for stealing. He eventually escaped, became a beggar, a petty thief, a professional burglar, and a drug smuggler. By age thirty-five he had been expelled from five countries and imprisoned in fifteen jails. Genet's sentence of life imprisonment was lifted only after a group of famous literary people petitioned the president of France for his release.

## Revolting Against Society

Genet used his plays to revolt against a society he felt had rejected him. Because he felt like an outsider, his characters are outcasts, people he admires and considers victims of society like murderers, thieves, prostitutes, prison inmates, maids, Arabs, and blacks. Genet's characters, like Said, the thief and traitor in *The Screens*, are like Genet—they enjoy being evil and outcasts, and they rebel against society. Genet suggests that their behavior is as important as what people accept as virtues in people.

Genet's plays are complex and hard to understand, but what people find most interesting about them is the way he designed them as rituals. He paints a picture of people engaging in ceremonies. They gesture, pose, and speak in a precise manner to give a sense of purpose and importance to what is really nonsensical, often criminal and evil, action. In this way Genet has probably come the closest to Antonin Artaud's concept of a theater of cruelty. Genet, as Artaud envisioned, also confronted people with their darker side. He designed his play *The Blacks* to be staged before an all-white audience by an all-black cast who wore white makeup. The characters perform a ritual reenactment of their resentment and feelings of revenge for the whites in order to confront the white audience with their racism.

The original set for *The Blacks* consisted of metal tubing arranged at different heights so it could be

*A scene between Mr. and Mrs. Smith from the original 1950 Paris production of* The Bald Soprano *by Eugene Ionesco. Courtesy French Cultural Services.*

*A scene from the Théâtre Gramont production, Paris, of* The Chairs *by Eugene Ionesco. Courtesy French Cultural Services.*

used as a staircase. When a performer finished his scene, he stayed on stage. Each performer announced his name and his role and transformed himself in front of the audience. The performers imitated the wind, the leaves, and a forest with their voices and their bodies.

In *The Screens* Genet wrote a political play that criticized the brutal way France was colonizing Algeria. Again Genet confronted audiences with their prejudices and their violent nature. Because France was still fighting with Algeria when Genet wrote *The Screens* it had to be produced in Germany; no one would stage it in France. In 1966 when it played in France it still enraged spectators. At one performance an audience threw seats at the stage and one actor had to be hospitalized.

## Actors and Production Style

Genet's characters love to perform, to pretend to be many people, and the performers who played these roles often wore layers of outlandish costumes and

*A scene from The Guthrie Theater production of* The Screens *by Jean Genet, with Jesse Borrego as Said, Ruth Maleczech as Said's Mother, and Lauren Tom as Leila, his wife. Photograph by Joe Gianetti. Courtesy The Guthrie Theater.*

sometimes high headdresses to hide their characters' true identity. In Genet's plays performers often wore masks under which their characters act out their dreams and desires, or they wore mask-like makeup that sometimes had tendons and veins drawn on it. The actors used unnatural gestures and distorted voices.

Genet confronted and shocked his audiences through his themes, his subjects, and his theatrical images. Roger Blin, as he did for Samuel Beckett, championed Genet's plays because he felt they had something important to offer.

All this adventurous work was taking place in tiny theaters in France at the same time that the Comédie Française was presenting the classic French plays and the boulevard theaters were staging entertaining plays. In England the commercial theaters in the West End of London were still offering comedies and other amusing entertainments to mostly wealthy audiences as they had done since the eighteenth century. The strict censorship of plays, which had been enforced by the Lord Chamberlain's office since 1737, kept British theater from exploring important issues and experimenting.

## CHANGES IN ENGLISH THEATER

The course of English theater began to change on the night of May 8, 1956. The right theater combined with the right director and the right playwright to start a renaissance in English playwriting, acting, directing, and stage design.

George Devine was an actor and the director of the English Stage Company, a group of actors who performed at the Royal Court Theatre in London. Devine was committed to discovering new playwrights and producing new English plays, and he advertised for original playscripts in a stage newspaper. John Osborne, a twenty-seven-year-old actor with no job or money, responded to the ad by submitting *Look Back in Anger*, a play that had been rejected by twenty-five managers and agents. Devine staged this play, which lashed out against the English establishment, including authority figures, the middle class, and traditional values.

In a realistic setting of a rundown one-room

apartment complete with double bed, bookshelves, ironing board, sink, kitchen table, and gas stove, the hero, Jimmy Porter, was often savage to his wife and best friend. Osborne used the character of Jimmy Porter to voice the anger, boredom, frustration, and desperation of many young English people.

Many regular theatergoers, members of the middle and upper classes, were horrified by the play. They disapproved of the crude language and missed the usual fashionable scenery. They declared that Jimmy Porter was not a fit character for the English stage. Osborne's play and the Royal Court Theatre, however, encouraged many young playwrights to write about the frustrations and fears of people and to explore social and political issues in their plays.

## New Playwrights—The "Angry Young Men"

Among the most noted of these new playwrights were Edward Bond, John Arden, David Story, and Arnold Wesker. Many of them came from working-class families, had left school at an early age, and earned their livings at odd jobs. Collectively they were known as the "angry young men" because in their plays they captured the rebellious mood that so many people were feeling. They protested against social and economic conditions. (England suffered economically and physically even after World War II.) The "angry young men" wrote about an entire class of people who had to struggle because they their basic material and emotional needs were not being met. These playwrights glorified characters who were nonconformists and misfits, often crude and rough.

The English stage no longer depicted only the lives of the privileged classes. Much of the new English drama was about the important issues of life. The message from the Royal Court Theatre was that the theater had to be about something. The Royal Court continued to encourage writers and brought back respect to realistic drama.

## George Devine

George Devine wanted playwrights to regard the Royal Court as a workshop where they could try, learn, fail, and grow. He held informal Saturday night

*A scene from the 1968 Asolo Center for the Performing Arts' production of* Look Back in Anger *by John Osborne, with Robert Britton as Jimmy, Charlotte Moore as Alison, and Anthony Heald as Cliff. Courtesy Asolo Center for the Performing Arts.*

get-togethers where aspiring playwrights and directors could exchange ideas and discuss problems. Devine instituted "Sunday Night Productions Without Decor" where young writers could see their plays produced for little money. Devine even included seasons of plays for young theatergoers and toured plays to schools.

## Joan Littlewood

The dedicated director Joan Littlewood also brought fresh and stimulating ideas to the English theater, especially after World War II. Littlewood was a talented teenage actress in the 1930s who gave up a secure career in the commercial theater to found the Theatre Workshop. Like Bertolt Brecht she believed that theater must contribute to the struggle for peace and progress. She hoped to make British theater an important force in society again by presenting plays meaningful to a working-class audience.

For years her group struggled, traveling by truck and playing in halls in working-class neighborhoods throughout England. The group survived on a diet of sausages and sometimes worked for no pay. They used what extra money they had to buy soap and toothpaste. In 1953 the group moved to a battered old theater in the East End of London, a working-class area. For years they worked to bring the people of this area back to the theater, and they brought the theater to the people, especially by staging special performances for schoolchildren.

Even though for several years the conditions were terrible (the group turned old clothes into costumes, scrounged material to build sets, rehearsed in ramshackle rooms, and made little money), writers and actors wanted to work with Littlewood. As one actress explained, she wasn't just going to rehearsals and learning her lines because Littlewood created a group that worked collectively to create their productions.

Littlewood wanted to present the dramas of new playwrights and she worked with young writers like Brendan Behan and the teenager Shelagh Delaney on developing their scripts. Instead of accepting a new play as a finished product Littlewood let everyone have input on the work. She wanted the playwright in the theater working with the actors to make the play come alive on stage.

## Brendan Behan

Several of Brendan Behan's plays were born at The Theatre Workshop. When rehearsals began for his play *The Quare Fellow*, which is set in a prison, instead of being given the script to read, the performers went on the roof of the theater, which looked like a prison yard, and imagined they were prisoners. The players improvised a lot, made up scenes, and only gradually the plot and text were introduced. In rehearsal the playwright had an opportunity to change lines and scenes that didn't work. In the same way the actors received lots of individual criticism and input on their work. The actors, playwright, and director explored together to find the right style

*Joan Littlewood (right) directing* Sparrows Can't Sing. *Courtesy Central Office of Information, London.*

for each play. Plays were changed and developed further even while they were being staged for audiences.

## Government Support for English Theater

The English theater was rejuvenated by directors like Littlewood and Devine, but another important factor brought the English theater to life again. The British government committed itself to assisting the arts by giving financial aid to artistic groups through the Arts Council of Great Britain. Parliament authorized local governments to set aside a percentage of tax money to support the arts, and cities and towns were urged to assist local theater companies financially.

It was now possible for theater groups to experiment with plays that might not be big hits or moneymakers because they didn't have to worry constantly about bankruptcy. Audiences were excited about many of the new theaters built outside of London, which did away with the proscenium arch stage. Some theaters featured versions of the Elizabethan thrust stage or open stage with the audience seated on three sides of a long, raised platform built against one wall of the auditorium. Theaters-in-the-round were also built. Also known as an arena stage, this is a circular stage that looks like a circus ring in which the audience is seated completely around the playing space. There were experiments with flexible stages, too, also known as adaptable or transformable stages. The staging and the audience area can be rearranged so that almost any type of setup can be made. The audience and actors can be placed in different relationships to each other. In 1951 the first entirely flexible theater was built at the University of Bristol in England. Theater artists in other countries had opportunities to work in these different types of theater spaces, too.

## THEATER ELSEWHERE IN EUROPE

### France

In France after World War II the government expanded theater outside of Paris into the rest of the country. The process was called *decentralization*. National dramatic centers each with its own director were established in large cities throughout France as were Permanent Troupes that toured and offered productions to people in towns and cities not close to a dramatic center. Both received financial assistance from the local government and the central government in Paris.

### Russia, Germany, and Scandinavia

In Russia, Germany, and the Scandinavian countries state-subsidized theaters located throughout their countries had already been established in the eighteenth century. The governments in these countries considered it their cultural responsibility to fund the arts because they felt the arts were an important part of the life of their people. Now, France and England were lending similar support to their theater artists and spreading their theaters out from their capital cities, Paris and London.

The period from the end of World War II to the present has been one of rebuilding, expansion, and experimentation in the European theater. While the playwrights, directors, and scenic designers who have emerged all have their own style, they have been influenced by the people and ideas that have come before them. Many outstanding theater artists have appeared in the European theater in the second half of the twentieth century. We can't explore all their work but we can meet some of the most exciting playwrights and directors whose work has had an influence on world theater since 1960.

# 10. EUROPEAN THEATER SINCE 1960: BREAKING DOWN BARRIERS

Germany was slow to recover from the devastation of World War II. Many theaters throughout the country had to be rebuilt and they were—large theaters for traditional drama and small theaters for experimental plays. The large theaters like The Schiller Theatre have stages with a proscenium arch and modern machinery, including revolving stages, rolling platforms, and elevators. The small theaters have a variety of stages—arena, thrust, and flexible. Since the 1960s the government has continued to subsidize these many theaters, and German theater is considered the best supported in the world.

## GERMAN DOCUMENTARY DRAMA

In the 1960s German playwrights were inspired by the plays and theories of Bertolt Brecht, especially the idea that theater should be political, and they wrote plays that are known as *documentary drama* or *theater of fact*. Playwrights took recent actual historical events and presented them in play form. The German playwrights used these plays to react against a contemporary event or to demand an explanation for why something happened as it did. Playwrights hoped that audiences who saw these plays would learn lessons from and question the past.

These documentary plays were based on factual reports. The dialogue often was taken from documents, statistics, speeches, letters, and transcripts, which were unedited and carefully selected to present a certain viewpoint.

### Peter Weiss and Rolf Hochhuth

Peter Weiss and Rolf Hochhuth were two of the most influential playwrights to write documentary dramas. Weiss went from an unknown playwright to an internationally famous one with his first play, known as *Marat/Sade*. In it Weiss combined elements from Brecht and Artaud. He took the histori-

cal figures Jean-Paul Marat who fought in the French Revolution and believed in social revolution, and the Marquis de Sade, who believed in the rights of the individual. He used the fact that Marat was stabbed in his bath, which he took often for an unbearable skin disease, and the fact that the Marquis de Sade, while imprisoned in a mental asylum for the insane and socially "difficult," wrote plays and directed the inmates in them. This information was the inspiration Weiss used to write *Marat/Sade*, in which Marat and Sade confront each other and debate their social and political philosophies in an 1808 French mental institution. At the same time the Marquis de Sade directs the lunatics in the asylum as they act out the historical events leading to Marat's assassination. The play ends with the inmates rioting and the confrontation between Sade and Marat unresolved.

The way Peter Weiss presented his play-within-a-play with the events of the French Revolution of 1793 reenacted in 1808 made audiences compare how people then and now resolve their political differences. Then they used the guillotine, now we use nuclear weapons. The setting of an insane asylum was used to mirror the violence and irrationality of today's world. Like Brecht, Weiss used the past to explore the present.

In 1965 Peter Weiss's documentary drama *The Investigation* was considered so important for Germans to gain an understanding of their history that it was produced in seventeen German theaters simultaneously. Weiss attempted to show who was to blame for the deaths of so many Jews in the extermination camp in Auschwitz, Poland during World War II. The play is an account of the trials of the Auschwitz concentration camp officials at the end of World War II, and it consists of excerpts from the transcripts of the Frankfurt War Crimes Trial. The play is composed of the testimony of officials and guards at Auschwitz, the denials of the people accused, and

*Scene from the 1990 Williamstown Theatre Festival production of* Marat/Sade *by Peter Weiss, directed by Paul Weidner. Photograph by Richard Feldman. Courtesy Williamstown Theatre Festival.*

*A scene from* The Deputy *by Rolf Hochhuth. Courtesy German Information Center/Owen Franken-GIC.*

the comments of the lawyers.

Rolf Hochhuth's documentary play *The Representative*, known in the United States as *The Deputy*, like his other plays *The Soldiers* and *Juristen*, caused great controversy, even demonstrations. Hochhuth researched the subject completely and kept to the facts when he wrote this eight-hour play in which a Jesuit priest confronts Pope Pius XII and accuses him of standing by and doing nothing while the Jewish people were being murdered. The play condemns the Pope for not helping even though he had to know that Adolf Hitler and the Nazis were arresting, deporting, and exterminating thousands of Jewish people. The characters in *The Deputy* are either from real life or modeled on them; the events pictured actually happened.

## RESPONSE TO UNREST WORLDWIDE

In the late 1960s and early 1970s stresses were felt in almost every country. Third world countries were struggling for survival. There were social and economic problems around the world. The superpowers, including the Soviet Union, the United States, China, and France were engaged in conflicts in Africa and Southeast Asia. Many individuals and groups started to question traditional values and conventions. Young students throughout Europe became politically aware and protested against established institutions. Their hostility exploded into violence in the streets of Paris in 1968, which became known as the "Events of May." People everywhere wanted to live by their own standards, to change what didn't agree with their views. Many voices wanted to be heard.

The theater responded to these events and feelings in numerous ways. Theater artists searched for a direct way to confront audiences with the political and social issues of the times. Brecht's work was very appealing. Artaud's theories appealed, too, because they expressed the spirit of that revolt against western civilization felt by young theater people. Artaud abandoned traditional forms of theater, broke down the dividing line between the actors and the audience, and used all the space in a non-traditional building, and so did many young theater people. Like

Artaud they found Oriental and Asian theater traditions attractive and used them in their work.

### Théâtre du Soleil

One exciting group that developed in France in the 1960s and has had a great impact on European theater is the Théâtre du Soleil (Theater of the Sun), directed by Ariane Mnouchkine. In the late 1960s and 1970s Théâtre du Soleil staged innovative productions, which they constructed out of the improvisations, group study, and discussions of the theater company. The 1969 production of *The Clowns* resulted after each actor developed the character of a specific clown and improvised scenes involving each clown. The final show was a series of improvisations and individual acts that included music, songs, and jokes.

All the members of the company share the responsibility to research, write scripts, and assist with the settings, design, costumes, and rehearsals. Ariane Mnouchkine wants everyone to assist in every facet of the production rather than make all the decisions herself. Each performer must also take a turn doing the menial tasks like sweeping the stage. From 1968 all the members of the company received the same salary.

### Environmental Theater

Théâtre du Soleil explored the political and social concerns they had in plays they created, which included elements from popular theater like songs, masks, acrobatics, clowning, and mime. They also used an entire space, surrounding and involving the audience. This style of production is known as *environmental theater*. All the space in a garage, loft, hall, or room is used to create the performance area, and the actors and the audience are in contact with each other during the show.

In 1970 Théâtre du Soleil moved to an unused factory called the Cartoucherie where weapons and ammunition were made during World War II. There they presented two of their most famous works, *1789* and *1793*, which treat the early years of the French Revolution. These plays combined the groups' political beliefs with exciting presentations. To create *1789* the actors studied the historical period and came to know it in great detail. They divided into small groups of four or five and searched for ways to present the many events of the time. At the end of each day's work the actors would have from ten to thirty improvisations and the entire company would watch each one and judge them. After months of such work the final play was created.

*1789* was a collage of eighteen improvised scenes, some very simple, others complex, that showed many different viewpoints of the Revolution. Some of the scenes showed the same event as it was perceived by different characters or classes of people. Other scenes used the actual words of historical characters.

The entire factory was used to stage the play. The whole company helped created the set, which consisted of five raised platforms connected by bridges or runways to form a square that surrounded the spectators. The audience stood during the performance and had to keep moving in one direction or another depending on where the action was happening. At times the action spilled over from the stage and into the audience.

The performance of *1789* built to the scene in which the people are about to take the Bastille, the French government's prison. Each performer placed himself at a different spot in the central area, gathered a small group of spectators around him, and described the storming of the Bastille as though he were describing it to French citizens of the time. Then a party would break out as the actors celebrated the overthrow of the government. The play ended with music, dancing, acrobats, wrestling—every amusement you might see at a fairground, and the spectators could join in the fun. At the end of the show many people didn't want to leave, and often they would stay and have lively discussions with the actors and each other until late in the evening, exploring the ways in which the events of the play paralleled conditions in their society.

Théâtre du Soleil staged two other plays, *1793* and *The Age of Gold*, which incorporated their political beliefs with French history in a novel performance style. For *The Age of Gold* in 1975 the group explored how society exploits and oppresses classes of people and individuals. The troupe wanted the au-

dience to feel a part of the action, to feel a relationship with the actors. They tried to create a performance in which every word, inflection, and gesture would be important, like signs that the spectators would immediately recognize and understand, as in Chinese and Japanese theater. A new environment was created in the factory space. Four large hollows were devised by piling tons of earth into large dunes. These were covered with matting and the audience sat in these slopes, moving from space to space as the actors invited them.

Théâtre du Soleil continues to explore and challenge what theater is. They have worked on reinterpreting Shakespeare's plays using Asian music and dance in their performances. In 1984 Americans had the opportunity to see Théâtre du Soleil at the Los Angeles Olympics.

## OTHER FRENCH THEATER GROUPS

Other theater groups in France from the late 1960s were dissatisfied with the commercial theaters, the national theaters in Paris and out, and the dramatic centers throughout the country. Some of these artists work in experimental drama studios that exist all over the country. Some groups model themselves after the work of Roger Planchon, who tried to attract working class audiences. Others chose to perform outside of traditional theater spaces in cafés and artists' centers. In 1967 Grand Magic Circus tried to appeal to all types of audiences in a very direct way by performing at parks, beaches, and hospitals. They improvised scenes, included popular elements like acrobatics, and even had audience members change roles with the performers.

## NEW DEVELOPMENTS IN ENGLISH THEATER

Many factors combined to make English theater vital and exciting in the last decades of the twentieth century—excellent playwrights, the rise of a *fringe* or alternative theater, regional theaters outside of London, the women's theater movement, and the work from three important theaters. One other momentous historical event changed the fate of English theater.

## The Theatre Act of 1968

After over 200 years, the Licensing Act of 1737 was reversed with The Theatre Act of 1968, and the Lord Chamberlain's role as theater censor was abolished. Pre-production censorship of plays to 1968 had been one of the main reasons that English playwriting remained traditional. Every play had to be submitted to the Lord Chamberlain's office and licensed before it could be staged. The Lord Chamberlain could request changes or cuts of words, sentences, even entire scenes. It was difficult for playwrights to deal with important human, social, and political issues in a realistic way when the censor was there to ban anything he thought might be objectionable. Playwrights were frustrated since the same subjects and plays could be performed on television with no censorship.

The English Stage Company at the Royal Court Theatre, which did produce plays that tried to deal seriously with contemporary problems, turned itself into a club theater admitting members only so they could stage unlicensed works, including many by John Osborne and Edward Bond. This system was similar to what Jacob Grein's Independent Theatre Society did to present Shaw's and Ibsen's plays at the beginning of the century.

A new freedom came with the Theatre Act of 1968. Many plays that had been banned were produced immediately. *Hair*, a rock musical that had been censored in England for its nudity and obscenities, was staged the day after censorship was abolished. *The Soldiers* by Rolf Hochhuth was produced. This play claimed that during World War II former Prime Minister Winston Churchill plotted to kill Polish General Wladyslaw Sikorski, who died in a plane crash. Before the Theatre Act of 1968 *The Soldiers* would not have been allowed on stage because plays weren't allowed to criticize public figures, heads of state, or members of the royal family, even if they were dead.

## The Fringe Theater

Many of the new playwrights, actors, and directors pursued their work in the fringe or alternative theater. In the fringe these artists could produce many plays even though they couldn't find opportunities for creative work in the West End, London's commercial theater district, because their work was too political or experimental. The groups in the fringe enjoyed their greatest popularity from 1968 to 1973.

The fringe groups had little money to work with even if they received small subsidies and grants from the government, so they worked hard for little pay. The Quipu Basement Theatre offered lunch-hour productions in the basement of a restaurant, and the performers often worked for no pay. They preferred that to not working in the theater at all. These groups mounted productions, usually short plays with small casts, little scenery, and simple lighting. They used unconventional buildings or spaces they could rent inexpensively like pubs, playgrounds, meeting halls, churches, tents, cellars, and attics. Roundhouse, a fringe group in London, used a massive old industrial building. The group Inter-Action, headed by the American Ed Berman, staged their play *Pisces* in a swimming pool. The audience sat around the edges of the pool and, at the end of the play, jumped into the water with the actors. The members of Inter-Action not only worked collaboratively to create their plays, as many of the fringe groups did, but they also lived together in a commune at Chalk Farm in London.

Many of these groups wanted to attract and play to audiences that didn't attend the theater. Often they did so by touring and going out to reach people. The Bubble Theatre Company staged plays in the parks in London. Inter-Action had a mobile theater called the Fun Art Bus, which staged plays for children at playgrounds. Many of these groups, like Théâtre du Soleil in France, explored new ways to set up the relationship between the performers and the audience. Some groups not only wanted to surround the audience, but they wanted to shock and confront them. In 1969 at a festival of fringe theater productions at the Royal Court Theatre, members of the Ken Campbell Roadshow smeared chocolate cake and eggs across the laps of the spectators.

Some of the fringe groups were political like Théâtre du Soleil, with all their members working for political action and change in society through their work. The company Red Ladder traveled to community centers where they presented plays about such issues as housing problems.

The fringe theater still exists with the help of small subsidies, as does the National Youth Theatre, which works with non-professional teenage performers. It offers excellent training and outstanding productions for youngsters in England. The greatest public funds go to The English Stage Company at the Royal Court Theatre, which continues to nurture aspiring young playwrights, The Royal Shakespeare Company, and The National Theatre.

## The National Theatre

England was one of the last European countries to establish a national theater unlike France, for example, which has had the Comédie Française since the seventeenth century. In 1963 Laurence Olivier, who had continued his career as a superb actor, became the first director of The National Theatre. The actors performed in several different theaters until The National Theatre's own building was completed in 1976.

The National Theatre offers a varied choice of plays and production styles, and many English and foreign directors are hired to work there. The National houses three auditoriums—a proscenium arch theater, an open stage, and a flexible stage on which new techniques and new or little known plays can be staged. The National also has many workshops and a hundred dressing rooms.

## The Royal Shakespeare Company

The Royal Shakespeare Company, considered Britain's foremost repertory company, moved to London's Barbican Centre for Arts and Conferences in 1982. The Centre is Western Europe's largest art complex. In the 1960s the Royal Shakespeare Company first gained a reputation for its experimentation, innovative techniques, and wide range of productions. Two of its most influential directors of the time were Peter Hall and Peter Brook.

## Peter Brook

Peter Brook staged his first production at age eighteen and became co-director of the Royal Shakespeare Company in 1962. Brook is the only director to have tested Antonin Artaud's theories for any length of time. Out of this experimental workshop in 1964, which also explored Bertolt Brecht's tech-

*Royal National Theatre, The National Theatre of Great Britain. Courtesy Royal National Theatre.*

*A scene from Peter Brook's production of* A Midsummer Night's Dream. *Courtesy of The Billy Rose Theatre Collection, The New York Public Library for the Performing Arts, Astor, Lenox and Tilden Foundations.*

niques, Brook created a shocking, visually exciting version of Peter Weiss's *Marat/Sade*.

In Brook's production Jean-Paul Marat argues with the Marquis de Sade while seated in a bathtub. Their debate is interrupted by the insane inmates who act out Marat's story and their own desires. During the scene in which the inmates act out the guillotining—chopping off heads—that was done during the French Revolution, the actors playing the inmates made metallic rasping noises to suggest the sound of a blade, and they poured buckets of red paint to suggest blood draining down. Other inmates jumped into a pit in the center of the stage so only their heads were seen piled up next to the guillotine. Brook created violent visual images that assaulted

the audience and expressed more than language alone could.

Brook continued to explore ways to relate the audience to the action of a play beyond using words. He worked to create new meaningful interpretations of Shakespeare's plays. In 1970 people marveled at his interpretation of *A Midsummer Night's Dream*. Brook used ideas from the Chinese circus, the *commedia dell'arte*, Brecht, Artaud, and Meyerhold. The original play takes place in a woodland where fairies and lovers meet. Instead of recreating this place, Brook chose to convey the play's theme of love and to make the play a celebration of the theater and performers. After seeing Chinese acrobats perform, Brook realized that their movement and leaps were the perfect image to convey the essence of what fairies are, rather than actors wearing wings or flimsy costumes, for example.

Audiences and critics talked for a long time about this production. The curtainless stage revealed a setting consisting of three high white walls—a bare white box with a floor of soft white matting. There were two white swinging doors in the back wall. Bright white lights, which the audience could see, lit the stage. Ladders led up the middle of the side walls where fifteen feet above the lower stage level was an upper gallery encircling the set.

The trees of the forest where the lovers wander consisted of lengths of coiled wire hung from massive steel fishing rods from the upper gallery. Also hanging down into the blank white space were ropes and trapezes. The chamber of Titania, queen of the fairies, was suggested by a trapeze covered with gigantic red ostrich feathers.

The audience watched as the performers conversed while swinging on the trapezes or climbing ladders, chased each other around the upper gallery, and dove for ropes that scooped them over the heads of other performers.

The upper narrow black balcony was an important part of the production. Not only did performers chase each other, but the actors who played the fairies could be seen moving the coils of wire to entangle the actors who played the lovers in the woods. The fairies made sounds and threw confetti from the balcony. Also, in full view of the audience, musicians created sound effects and played an accompaniment on bongos, autoharps, and tubular bells. When an actor needed a prop, it was thrown to him from the balcony. Nothing was hidden from the audience. The lovers were awakened in the woods by the ringing of an alarm clock displayed by one of the property men on the upper stage.

Brook's images were unique. The fairy king Oberon and his aide Puck dispensed love juice from a magic flower, but it wasn't done with a pretend flower. Instead, a spinning, humming, silver plate was tossed back and forth between clear plastic wands.

The play was a joyous celebration that took place on several levels and in mid-air. At the end the performers jumped down into the auditorium and smiled and shook hands with everyone they could reach as they walked past. Many people left the theater with the feeling that they had shared in a celebration.

## The International Centre of Theatre Research

Peter Brook began a new phase in his work in 1971 when he moved to Paris and became director of The International Centre of Theatre Research. The Centre, first located in a former tapestry factory, is a workshop where actors, writers, and directors from cultures all over the world can experiment and create theater pieces. Brook works to discover a form of theater that will be immediately understandable to any human, no matter what his culture or language. Since Brook doesn't believe that words communicate much, he has searched to create a new theatrical language that uses sounds, made-up words, gestures, movements, and other visual means to relate the audience to the action.

One of The Centre's first projects was presented at the Shiraz Festival at Persepolis in Iran. The actors retold an old legend on a mountaintop in a language they had invented called Orghast. In 1972 The Centre members went on a three-month journey through small towns in five countries in Africa and improvised scenes using only the actors and a carpet that defined the playing space. In one market in Algeria a pair of heavy, dusty boots became the focus for an improvised scene.

## Experimentation Continues

Peter Brook's experimentation into what is theater continues. His actors have performed for deaf children and patients in mental institutions, on cliffs, in pits, on street corners, even at a zoo. In 1974 the Centre moved to Théâtre des Bouffes du Nord in Paris, a dilapidated, decaying nineteenth century theater, which was ready for demolition. Brook left the theater much as he found it, with towering walls that are charred, streaked by rain, scarred and pitted, but also glowing red, and floors that are damaged. The playing area has no curtain and is on the same level as the audience, offering a vast, open, empty space that can become anyplace. In this theater

Brook has attempted to "reunite the community, in all its diversity, within the same shared experience."

Peter Brook has been hailed as the most important, influential, thoughtful, creative theater director in the past fifty years. He always seeks to do new or old material in a fresh way and never considers a production finished but always open to further study and change. Brook brings together many theater styles, performers, and playing spaces. He attempts to appeal to all kinds of audiences.

### The Mahabharata

One of Brook's most recent productions, which many have praised as his masterpiece, is *The Mahabharata*. This is a nine and a half hour-long play based on the longest work of literature, the epic poem of Hinduism written in India between 200 BC and 200 AD. Brook worked on creating *The Mahabharata* for twelve years. During that time Brook's multinational company traveled to India several times, where they created the scenes. They dedicated themselves to many years of work and struggle for this project. The writer Jean-Claude Carrière turned the actors' experiences into a text, writing and rewriting each scene as he saw it evolve with the performers.

*The Mahabharata* has been staged around the world in a variety of spaces, from a rock quarry on the banks of a river to a clay stage. It is the tale of gods and demons, of quarreling dynasties and earth-shaking wars. It is done by moving quickly from tale to tale, from place to place, skipping through time. Lengths of Indian fabric were laid on the bare earth to suggest the changing location of the play. The actors used their bodies as instruments to tell the tale. There were no sets, only objects. Sticks and bamboo screens were used to suggest bows and arrows, war machines, beds, tents, and shields.

The main images evoked in the play are of fire, water, and earth. To a background of music by six musicians using dozens of Oriental and African instruments, audiences saw fires blazing to evoke the gods or to call forth enemies. In one scene a snake-like fire ignited in a pool of real water. Actors waded in the pools and rivers of real water. There were many memorable images in this play: chariot wheels stuck in real mud, armies fought by torchlight, and a stunningly gowned goddess carried in on an elephant's back made from the actors' bodies.

## OTHER THEATER ARTISTS

Peter Brook wasn't the only dynamic theater artist to emerge in England in the last decades of this century. Peter Nichols, Simon Gray, Tom Stoppard, Peter Shaffer, Ann Jellicoe, Howard Brenton, and David

*A scene from Missouri Repertory Theatre's 1990 production of Peter Shaffer's* Amadeus, *directed by Dennis Rosa. Photograph by Larry Pape. Courtesy Missouri Repertory Theatre.*

*A scene from Missouri Repertory Theatre's 1990 production of Peter Shaffer's* Amadeus, *directed by Dennis Rosa with Benjamin Evett as Amadeus. Photograph by Larry Pape. Courtesy Missouri Repertory Theatre.*

*A scene from South Coast Repertory's 1989 production of* A Chorus of Disapproval *by Alan Ayckbourn, with Joe Spano, David Schramm, and Caroline Smith. Photography by Ron Stone. Courtesy South Coast Repertory.*

Hare are just a few of the British playwrights who help keep English theater among the best in the world. Peter Shaffer has written about the search for God in plays that include *Equus, The Royal Hunt of the Sun*, and *Amadeus*. Alan Ayckbourn has become England's most popular playwright, writing entertaining farces about married life, including *How the Other Half Loves* and *Bedroom Farce*. Ayckbourn depicts the English middle class—the same people who come to see his plays—as money hungry, materialistic people whose morals are lacking. But the playwright who has gained the greatest reputation from critics is Harold Pinter, whose plays are often grouped with those of the absurdists.

## HAROLD PINTER

Harold Pinter has created his own vivid theatrical images to portray people who are isolated, unable to communicate with others, and frightened by a world that seems impossible to understand. In Pinter's plays, which include *The Birthday Party, The Dumb Waiter, The Caretaker, The Room*, and *The Homecoming*, the characters seem to be involved in ordinary events, but gradually there is a feeling of mystery, dread, terror, or violence in the everyday situations. It's not always clear what the characters should be afraid of or what they're trying to defend themselves against, but the feeling is there. In *The Room* the character Rose regards the room as her only refuge against whatever is beyond the room. The action in Pinter's plays is never explained, and you're not sure why characters do what they do. In *The Birthday Party* a loser named Stanley lives in a boarding house. Two men come to his room, menace him, interrogate him, then take him away.

The characters talk without saying what they mean and there are long silences and pauses that seem sinister and full of meaning. In *The Caretaker*, audiences sense how difficult it is for humans to communicate and why they end up isolated. In the play, a man brings an old tramp to stay in his house, but the man's brother harasses the tramp and the tramp tries to pit the brothers against each other. The tramp is told to leave.

Harold Pinter, like Samuel Beckett and Eugene

*Scene from Steppenwolf Theatre company's 1989 production of Harold Pinter's* The Homecoming, *with Rick Snyder as Sam and Randall Arney as Teddy; directed by Jeff Perry. Photo by Michael Brosilow. Courtesy Steppenwolf Theatre Company.*

Ionesco, hasn't offered explanations for his plays. In 1967 after seeing *The Birthday Party* on Broadway in New York City, a woman wrote a letter to *The New York Times* asking Harold Pinter to explain the meaning of his play. He replied by asking her the meaning of her letter.

## WOMEN PLAYWRIGHTS

Thanks to the feminist movement, small regional theaters, and women's theater groups, more women playwrights have emerged in the European theater since the 1970s. In France Lilian Atlan has received the Légion d'Honneur, a tribute reserved for French individuals who are considered "National Treasures." Caryl Churchill of England is an internation-

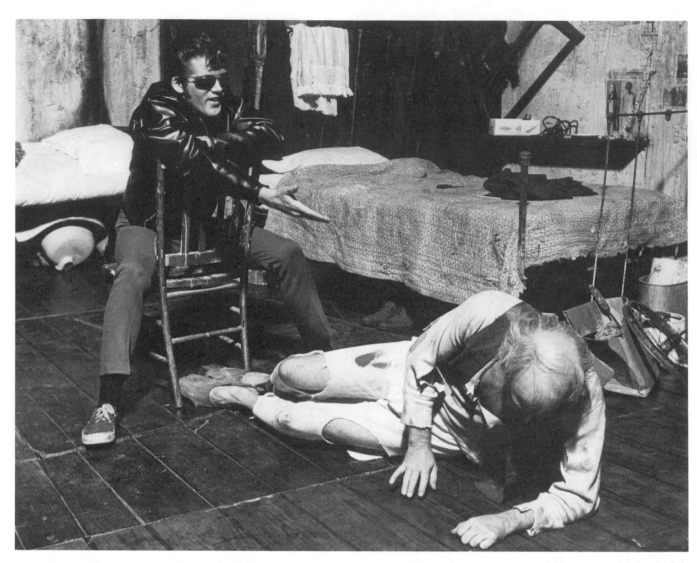

*Scene from a 1968 production of* The Caretaker *by Harold Pinter, with Macon McCalman and Anthony Heald. Courtesy Asolo Center for the Performing Arts.*

*Scene from a Berkshire Theatre Festival production of* Cloud 9 *by Caryl Churchill, directed by Michael Greif, with Jay P. Goede as Betty/Edward and Rafael Clements as Harry Bagley/Martin. Photograph by Walter Scott. Courtesy Berkshire Theatre Festival.*

ally respected playwright who writes about how social and economic forces affect people's relationships with each other. In *Fen* she portrays female farm workers who try to cope with their low wages and unhappy lives. In her most popular play, *Cloud 9*, Churchill explores the social forces that steer people into behaving according to stereotyped roles for men and women. Women directors have also become an important force in British theater recently.

## JERZY GROTOWSKI'S ACHIEVEMENTS

European theater from the 1960s isn't just the story of theater in Germany, France, and England. In a list of the ten most important theatrical achievements of the 1960s, *Time* magazine listed Polish theater artist Jerzy Grotowski's work as number one. Grotowski's exploration into the art of acting has been the most intense since that of Konstantin Stanislavsky. In the 1960s Grotowski wanted to answer the question, "What is theater?" After much experimentation he developed the concept of the *Poor Theatre*. He eliminated everything he felt the theater could do without—sets, machinery, costumes, makeup, lighting effects, and stages. What was left was the actor and the relationship between the actor and the audience.

Much of Grotowski's work is research rather than rehearsals for a production. In his Laboratory Theatre in Poland Grotowski's select group of performers dedicated themselves to intensive training sessions that went on for years. Grotowski developed a variety of techniques and physical exercises that enabled the actors to gain control of their entire bodies, from their breathing to their leg muscles. In a performance, they would become fine-tuned instruments. The actors did physical exercises for two to three hours every day. These methods also were designed to help actors confront whatever might be blocking their creative process. During a performance the actors could transform themselves as the production required. They would not use makeup or costumes to distinguish their characters or to show changes in their roles. Instead, they had to transform themselves through their posture, movement, voice, and facial expressions.

### The "Holy Actor"

Grotowski developed the concept of the *holy actor*. In front of spectators, each performer was expected to reveal or give of herself freely, to show herself exactly as she was. In a performance the actor, by hiding nothing, revealed his or her inner self and aroused a sense of wonder in people.

According to Grotowski theater was supposed to be holy, too, like a religious experience. The audience members were participants in a ritual. A production was like a group celebration in which the actors and the spectators confronted themselves and came to a better understanding of themselves and their world. To achieve his goal of crossing the "frontiers between you and me... To find a place where a communion becomes possible," Grotowski

*A scene from* Apocalypsis cum figuris *at Jerzy Grotowski's Polish Laboratory Theatre. Courtesy KaiDib Films International, Glendale, California.*

*A scene from* Apocalypsis cum figuris *at Jerzy Grotowski's Polish Laboratory Theatre. Courtesy KaiDib Films International, Glendale, California.*

eliminated obstacles that prevented the relationship from forming. He limited the number of spectators, sometimes to only twenty people, so the actors could establish a dialogue with them. He had the actors and spectators share a common space rather than be divided by a proscenium arch, and he arranged the spectators in such a way that they would have to react. He also decided ahead of time what viewpoint he wanted the audience to have, what type of relationship he wanted between actor and audience, and arranged them accordingly. For Grotowski's version of *Doctor Faustus* the entire space where the production took place became a monastery dining hall and the audience was seated at long tables as if they were guests at a banquet. As they entered, Faustus, already seated in the center of the head table, invited them to take their place as guests. The actor in his role as Faustus sat with them and related stories about his life.

Many of Grotowski's productions were acclaimed worldwide, including *Akropolis*, *The Constant Prince*, and *Apocalypsis cum figuris*. In *Akropolis* the spectators were seated separately and randomly throughout the hall where the action took place. The actors, wearing sacking and wooden clogs, used a pile of rusty stovepipes, a bathtub, a wheelbarrow, a hammer, and nails heaped on a platform to build a structure among the spectators. This structure represented a Nazi gas chamber. They used their voices for shrieks, raspy whispers, and chants, and their movements were carefully orchestrated to become symbolic.

*Apocalypsis cum figuris*, Grotowski's most outstanding work, took over three years to develop and continued to evolve for the next twelve years. In one of its presentations twenty-five spectators entered the darkened playing area with the actors one hour before the performance and sat on the floor. Two naked spotlights positioned against and pointing up one of the walls provided all the lighting. The actors conveyed this tale of the human race (which had evolved through their improvisations and acting exercises) without scenery, with no specific costumes. They used few props—a pail of water, a knife, candles, and bread. The actors' speech was limited to what was required to reinforce the symbolic meaning of the action.

Since 1970 Jerzy Grotowski's work has moved away from the theater into special projects and research in which the creative process is the creative result. What the participants in Grotowski's workshops or meetings do is the end result. The performers and spectators are one and the same.

## CHANGES IN EUROPEAN THEATER ELSEWHERE

Spain, Italy, and many Eastern European countries, including Russia and Czechoslovakia, have suffered censorship in their theaters. Since the late 1980s, however, Europe has undergone dramatic changes that are having an impact on the theater. In Russia Soviet authorities were censoring productions until the mid-1980s. Only The Taganka Theatre, under the courageous director Yuri Lyubimov, staged exciting plays with unusual production techniques in spite of being hounded by bureaucrats, the police, and censors.

### Yuri Lyubimov

For many years Lyubimov got away with commenting on Soviet society because he was very popular with audiences. He had to be subtle, though. Using symbols in his plays, he indirectly exposed police abuses, suppression of religious thought, censorship, and the use of psychiatric wards for political prisoners. In Lyubimov's production of *Hamlet*, the curtain was used to represent the Soviet government. During the play the curtain moved like a monster, swirled around the characters, and moved toward the audience. Symbols of power and oppression, including swords and goblets, were placed in the folds of the curtain.

Lyubimov walked a fine line with the censors, and in 1984 he was dismissed from The Taganka Theater after twenty years as artistic director. He was stripped of his Soviet citizenship and declared a nonperson. Lyubimov's story, until recently, would have ended with him directing plays in Europe and the United States. However, in 1985 Mikhail Gorbachev became secretary, or head, of the Communist Party and under his policy of *glasnost*, or openness,

*A scene from Center Stage's production of* The Increased Difficulty of Concentration *by Vaclav Havel, directed by Stan Wojewodski, Jr.; John Hutton as Karel Kriebl and Carolyn McCormick as Dr. Anna Balcar. Photo by Richard Anderson. Courtesy Center Stage.*

many restrictions on theater artists have ended. In May 1988 Yuri Lyubimov became the first prominent banished Soviet artist to return to the Soviet Union. He is directing at The Taganka Theatre again.

## In Czechoslovakia

Theater artists in Czechoslovakia were starting to create new and exciting productions until the Soviets invaded the country in 1968. During the next few years actors, playwrights, and directors whose political records were not totally in line with the Communist Party were removed from their work. Some were imprisoned, exiled, or banned. Many of them survived by working in the sewers or washing windows.

The Czech theater, like the Russian theater, remained extensive, but only plays that supported the Communist Party were approved. Small theater

companies did try to continue experimenting and presenting plays that criticized the government even though they were constantly monitored, plays were banned, and theaters were closed.

## Vaclav Havel

One of the playwrights whose work was banned was Vaclav Havel. From the time of the Soviet invasion he wrote, spoke out, and protested on behalf of human rights in Czechoslovakia. In 1977 he co-authored Charter 77, a radical proposal to restore human rights in his country. From that time he was investigated, searched, interrogated, put on trial, imprisoned, sent to labor camps and prison hospitals, but he continued to write plays.

In November 1989 Havel and thousands of theater artists from traditional and experimental companies united to change the repressive conditions in their country. All theater workers went on strike and stopped their performances until major changes were made in the government. Most theaters stayed open for meetings and political discussions between theater artists and the Czech citizens. Actors and directors went to factories and farms to persuade workers and farmers to join forces against the existing government. The people stood firm, won the revolution, and made Vaclav Havel president of Czechoslovakia. People acknowledge that without the intense activity of theater artists, the Czech revolution would not have been won.

Censorship of plays and productions was abolished, and since the revolution Czechs have been able to see Vaclav Havel's banned plays. Not surprisingly, in many of Havel's plays the main character is a political dissident caught in the grip of a repressive government.

Theater artists in the Soviet Union and in Czechoslovakia are unsure what direction their work will take. The traditional theaters no longer have to present plays that reflect the beliefs of the Communist Party. Experimental theaters don't have to concentrate on presenting work that revolts against the government. Now they can explore theater for its own sake or for any other purpose.

# 11. WITH OR WITHOUT A CURTAIN: EUROPEAN THEATER TODAY

No one knows what the future holds for the theater, not only in the former Soviet Union (now the Unified States) and Czechoslovakia, but in all of Europe, because of the dramatic political, social, and economic changes that are occurring. In Eastern Europe, Communist governments have collapsed in countries such as Poland and Romania. Western Europe is undergoing changes too. After forty-five years as two separate nations East and West Germany were reunited on October 3, 1990. By January 1, 1993 the twelve member nations of the Common Market, including England, Denmark, France, and Italy, will become a closer knit community when they begin allowing the free flow of money, people, and goods between their countries. The theater will change to reflect this new world. One delegate at the 1990 meeting of the USSR Center of the International Theatre Institute stated that European theater is at "a moment of beginning."

## A GROWING THEATER

What is certain is that there is and will be an incredible variety of theater in Europe and around the world. In Russia alone there are almost 700 professional theaters and 300 to 500 new small theaters have opened since 1988. In Germany there are almost 200 repertory troupes in over 100 cities. Each troupe stages up to twenty-five productions every year.

There are realistic and political plays, comedies, classical plays, plays that entertain, shock, or provoke, and plays that are rituals. Plays are improvised or carefully rehearsed, created by one individual or through collaboration. A director can faithfully interpret a playwright's work or reinterpret it, perhaps discovering new meaning in a well-known play. A director can stage a drama realistically, symbolically, in one style, or in a mixture of styles from many times and cultures. She can use elements from popular, Asian, Oriental, or Shakespearean theater, for example. She can stage a play simply, with only a few props, or elaborately with lavish sets, costumes, and visual effects.

Theater happens everywhere there are people, by groups large and small. In some theaters different people are hired for each individual production. In many other theaters in Europe the same theater artists work together on many different productions. They present different plays each night. This is known as the repertory system. Theater takes place in buildings of all types and sizes, national, state-run, government-supported theaters, in municipal centers and commercial, regional, private, and experimental theaters. It happens in schools, community centers, and rural villages. Plays are produced indoors on proscenium, thrust, arena, theater-in-the-round, and flexible stages. Theater happens outdoors, in parks, at playgrounds, on mountaintops.

## THEATER FESTIVALS

The best way to sample the theater of several countries is to attend one of the many theater festivals held around the world from England to Germany, from Turkey to Japan. At these festivals, plays, past and present, from several nations, are presented in one city or center for several days or weeks. The Edinburgh International Festival in Scotland, which has met annually since 1947, is the leading festival of theater, dance, music, and opera. In the late 1980s over 11,000 performances were offered in the fringe or experimental theater portion of the three-week festival. If you attended The New York International Festival of the Arts in 1991, you sampled plays from England, the Soviet Union, Yugoslavia, Sweden, Brazil, Spain, Poland, Zimbabwe, and the United States.

## CHILDREN'S THEATER FESTIVALS

You can also sample children's theater from around the world, theater performances given by adult professional or amateur actors for young people, at festivals like the Seattle International Children's Festival in Seattle, Washington, and the Philadelphia International Theatre Festival for Children in Philadelphia, Pennsylvania. Or you can travel to the Theatre Festival sponsored by ASSITEJ, the international association of theaters for children and youth, which has members in about forty countries. At the nine-day 1990 Theatre Festival ASSITEJ held in Stockholm, Sweden participants could, at three different times each day, choose from three to four different plays presented at fifteen locations. In addition to sponsoring international and local festivals, ASSITEJ helps children's theater companies tour from one country

*TIEBreak touring theatre in 'Singing in the Rainforest' at The Natural History Museum, London. Photograph by Derek Adams. Copyright: The Natural History Museum.*

to another.

According to Rose Marie Moudoues, Secretary General of the French Center of ASSITEJ, it's too soon to tell the consequences the political changes in Eastern Europe will have on children's theater. Like theater for adults in Europe, however, there is a wide variety of children's theater in countries including Germany, France, Czechoslovakia, the Unified States, and the Scandinavian countries. Sweden is the most active and innovative European country in children's theater where troupes like the world-reknowned Unga Klara company tour extensively. Unga Klara gears their plays to the concerns and needs of young people, and they are noted for the high quality of their productions. The Unga Klara company created and staged *Medea's Children*, a play about young people's perception of divorce. It became the most performed children's play in Europe during the 1980s. Unga Klara also first presented *Liquor*, about children and alcoholic parents, and *A Good Girl*, about a teenager with anorexia.

## CHILDREN'S THEATER IN THE UNIFIED STATES (SOVIET UNION)

Children's theater is an old tradition in the Unified States where, until the changes under Mikhail Gorbachev, theater was used to educate and indoctrinate children in the beliefs of Communism. Today there are almost 200 children's and puppet theaters and many children's troupes have their own theaters and tour their plays. The leading troupes for young audiences include The Soviet Theatre for Young Spectators, the Central Children's Theatre of Moscow, and the Yaroslavl Theatre for Young Spectators. These children's theater groups have great respect for the intelligence of the youngsters who attend their plays and offer them complex, fascinating, high quality dramas including political plays. Many of the dramas offered are based on works by writers and poets whose material has been banned until recently.

## CHILDREN'S THEATER IN BRITAIN

In Britain there are many professional theater companies that work primarily or only for children and

*A scene from Teatro dell'angolo of Italy's production for children,* Robinson and Crusoe. *Courtesy The Annenberg Center's 7th Philadelphia International Theatre Festival for Children, University of Pennysylvania.*

teenagers. There are also many Theatre-in-Education (TIE) companies of professional performers who work with different age groups from five to nineteen years old in schools, colleges, and youth clubs. A TIE company often spends a half day or more working in-depth with a group of thirty to forty young people with the children participating in the work.

## EUROPEAN THEATER IN THE FUTURE?

What the theater in Europe and the rest of the world will be like in the future is impossible to predict. As Eugene Ionesco said, "the theater, of course, changes, for the theater is life." But some things about the theater, all theater, will not change. The theater will always need courageous people like Yuri Lyubimov, Vaclav Havel, and Vsevelod Meyerhold; people with vision like Adolphe Appia and Antonin Artaud; innovators like David Garrick and Bertolt Brecht; and people who challenge what theater is like Alfred Jarry, Ariane Mnouchkine, Jerzy Grotowski, and Peter Brook. The theater will always need these and many other dedicated people like Konstantin Stanislavsky, Jacques Copeau, Sir Laurence Olivier, and Joan Littlewood. Everyone's role in the theater is important. The performers, playwrights, directors, stage hands, costumers, set designers, ushers, audiences—all contribute to the continuation of and to the history of the theater.

*A scene from Diablo Mundo of Argentina's production for children,* Memories, Dreams and Illusions. *Courtesy The Annenberg Center's 7th Philadelphia International Theatre Festival for Children, University of Pennsylvania.*

# GLOSSARY

**Actor-manager**—A person who ran his own theater, hired the performers, and staged and starred in plays he selected or that were written for him.

**"Angry young men"**—Collective term for a group of young English playwrights in the 1950s, whose plays captured the rebellious mood so many people were feeling. Through their plays these writers protested against the social and economic conditions of the time.

**Apron**—The large open platform that extended in front of the proscenium arch and into the auditorium, particularly in seventeenth and eighteenth century theaters.

**Avant-garde**—Refers to experimental theater in France from the late nineteenth century.

**Backdrop**—A scene painted on canvas and hung at the back of the stage.

**Ballad opera**—Versions of popular plays, often about a current issue, interspersed with songs. Ballad opera was popular in eighteenth century England.

**Biomechanics**—Term coined by Russian director Vsevolod Meyerhold. It refers to the method he developed for training his actors, which allowed them to control every movement and gesture they made to express emotions.

**Border**—Painted piece of scenery hung from the top of the stage.

**Border lights**—A row of lights along the front of the stage floor to provide illumination.

**Bourgeois tragedy (or domestic tragedy)**—A play about middle-class characters with settings such as counting houses and shops. In these plays the problems and values of the middle class are portrayed. First introduced in England by George Lillo in the early eighteenth century.

**Box set**—Stage setting created when the sides, or flats, of the stage are enclosed to form a room with three walls. First used in the early nineteenth century.

**Breeches part**—Role in which a woman or girl wearing male clothing plays the part of a man.

**Claque**—People hired to applaud, to sway audience opinion at a performance. Many claques were used in European cities, especially in Spain, France, and Italy in the eighteenth and nineteenth centuries.

**Cloak-and-sword drama**—Type of drama popular in Spain during the sixteenth and seventeenth centuries. They are stories of love, romance, adventure, intrigue, and honor, centering on the everyday lives of aristocratic and middle-class gentlemen. Derives its name from the clothing worn by men in these plays, which included a circular cape and sword.

**Comédie larmoyante**—Literally "tearful comedy," this type of play centered on cultured, educated, middle-class heroes and heroines who suffer misfortunes and are persecuted but finally have all their problems resolved happily by the play's end. Comédie larmoyante was created in eighteenth century France.

**Commedia dell'arte**—Literally "comedy of professional artists," it was the popular theater of the Italian Renaissance and the first theater with professional artists in organized companies. Actors played character types, wore masks, and improvised most of the play on simple platforms.

**Constructivism**—Created by Russian director Vsevolod Meyerhold, an abstract set which combined a variety of the following: stairs, ladders, ramps, turning wheels, platforms, springboards, and trapezes. Nothing was hidden, including struts and bolts. The set was functional, a machine for acting.

**Cup-and-saucer dramas** — Plays by Englishman Tom Robertson in the nineteenth century, these centered on the contemporary lives of ordinary people and included little incidents to give real-life touches to each play.

**Dadaism (or dada)** — Theater movement around the time of World War I, created under the leadership of Tristan Tzara. The Dadaists created a senseless and meaningless theater to reflect what they felt was the meaningless and insane world that produced World War I. Their theater consisted of programs, spontaneous and illogical collages of several things happening at once. They were often bizarre and shocking, consisting of anything that popped into the creator's mind.

**Decentralization** — In France, a process by which the government expanded theater outside the capital city of Paris into the rest of the country after World War II.

**Director** — The person who controls and unifies every aspect of a production. The person who creates the performance by imposing a point of view on the play.

**Documentary drama (or theater of fact)** — Plays created in Germany in the 1960s that took actual recent historical events and presented them in play form to react against a contemporary event or to demand an explanation for why something happened as it did.

**"Le drame bourgeois"** — Created in eighteenth century France, this was a type of play about the everyday life and problems of the middle class.

**Dream play** — Plays written by Swede August Strindberg at the turn of the twentieth century in the form of dreams to show people's states of mind, to show how they perceive the world.

**Elevator stage** — A stage divided into sections. Each section can be set at a different level, or an elevator can be used to raise heavy objects from beneath the stage.

**Emotion memory** — An acting exercise or aid developed by Russian director Konstantin Stanislavsky in which a performer takes a dramatic situation he must play but is unfamiliar with and relates it to a similar emotional situation from his own life. He can recall the similar situation when he must portray the character's situation.

**Environmental theater** — Theater in which the entire space is used. The actors and audience are in contact with each other during the performance, with the actors surrounding or involving audience members.

**Epic theater** — A theater style invented by German Erwin Piscator and further developed by German Bertolt Brecht. Epic theater was used as a tool to entertain and to teach, to change people's attitudes and encourage them to improve society. The plays in epic theater are episodic and include songs, dance, slides, and film.

**Expressionism** — Theater style that developed in Germany about 1910 and peaked in 1917-18. Playwrights tried to create visual images that expressed their fears and horror at the technological, mechanized world of the time. Acting and sets were distorted and unrealistic.

**Flat** — A light wood frame covered with canvas or fabric, it is often painted to resemble part of a wall and can be arranged on stage as part of the scenery.

**Flexible stage (or Adaptable or Transformable stage)** — The stage and audience area can be rearranged so that almost any type of setup can be made.

**Fringe (or Alternative theater)** — Found in England from the 1960s on, this type of theater produced short plays on small budgets, with small casts, little scenery, and simple lighting in unconventional buildings and spaces.

**Green room** — Furnished area backstage, painted green in the eighteenth century, where men from the audience could meet the female performers between appearances on stage.

**Holy actor**—Concept developed by Jerzy Grotowski of Poland in which each performer reveals or gives of himself freely, shows himself exactly as he is.

**Independent theater**—Also known as art theater, little theater, and experimental theater, this is a theater that is not commercial or government supported but privately subsidized by membership fees and donations. First appeared in the 1880s when André Antoine opened the Théâtre Libre in France. Traditionally, these theaters stage controversial plays that other theaters won't produce.

**Lazzi**—In commedia dell'arte, these were jokes—stunts, gestures, witty comments, and speeches—that had little to do with the play but added humor.

**"Legitimate" drama**—Term first coined in eighteenth century England, it referred to plays that were legal—licensed by the Lord Chamberlain. These included the tragedies and sentimental and witty comedies presented at the two licensed theaters in London during the eighteenth century—Drury Lane and Covent Garden.

**Limelight**—Invented in the late nineteenth century, this was an extremely bright spotlight that could focus attention on a certain acting area or character.

**Living light**—Term coined by Swiss scenic and lighting designer Adolphe Appia who suggested that light is a character or an integral part of a production, expressing set and mood, and blending the scene and the actors.

**Long run**—Keeping a production playing for as long as there are audiences who will come to see it. The long run came to replace the repertory system in which the play was changed each evening.

**Lord Chamberlain**—From 1737 to 1968 this was the individual who read, censored, and licensed all plays in England before they could be performed.

**The magic "If"**—An acting exercise developed by Russian director Konstantin Stanislavsky as an aid for actors to perform in the new realistic style, to find an inner justification for their actions on stage.

Actors asked themselves, "If I were this person faced with this situation, what would I do?" and used their responses in their roles.

**Mansion**—In medieval drama, a miniature room with no wall in front, housing simple props and furniture. It was used as an acting area.

**Melodrama**—Literally "melody drama" or "play with music." Originally, plays spoken to background music that expressed the emotions of the scene. A hero or heroine is pursued by a villain, but ultimately the hero escapes and the villain is defeated.

**Naturalism**—Plays first introduced by Émile Zola in France at the end of the nineteenth century, which reproduced a specific environment and showed characters struggling in this world. These plays were written to examine, criticize, and change problems in society.

**Neoclassical rules**—Rules for writing plays established by the French in the seventeenth century and (supposedly, but inaccurately) based on Greek plays. According to the rules, each play must be divided into five acts, be written in verse, and have only one action or main story that occurs in a single location in one day. The characters could only be kings and nobles; the themes must be important issues.

**Opera**—Theatrical form developed by the Italians in the 1590s in which a story is told through words sung to a musical accompaniment. Opera relies on music, spectacular sets, costumes, and mechanical devices.

**Panorama**—A long cloth on which a continuous scene was painted. Especially popular in nineteenth century melodramas.

**Pantomime**—A mixture of mime—silent acting—dance, and music which, in eighteenth century England, included a comic story line and featured the adventures of Harlequin, a funny and clever fellow who gets himself into trouble and out again.

**Play-within-a-play**—Term often associated with the plays of Italian Luigi Pirandello, in which actors play the part of actors playing characters.

**Poor Theater** — Concept developed by Polish director Jerzy Grotowski, a type of theater eliminating everything that is not needed for a performance, including, according to Grotowski, sets, machinery, costumes, makeup, lighting, and stage. What is left is the actor and the relationship between performer and audience.

**Presentational playhouse** — Term first used in reference to the playhouse fashioned by French director Jacques Copeau in the early twentieth century. Copeau's stark theater had a permanent setting — a single background which could be altered to stage any play.

**Proscenium arch** — The large "picture frame" that divides the acting area or stage from the audience.

**Realism** — Born in the late nineteenth century, a style of theater that includes scenery consisting of recognizable surroundings in box sets, stories that are probable, with characters from everyday life who are treated truthfully. The acting is based on the way people really talk and behave.

**Repertory system** — System in which a theater stages different plays every night or in a rotation on a regular basis.

**Revolving stage** — Type of stage that allows fast and smooth scene changes. A huge circle is cut out of the stage floor and mounted on wheels so it can be turned. Different settings are placed back to back, and each appears in the opening of the proscenium arch in turn as the stage floor revolves.

**Rolling platform stage** — Settings are mounted on a large platform offstage and then moved on stage by rollers set in tracks.

**Selective realism** — Staging in which just enough props and scenery are put on stage to suggest a setting. For example, an oversized bed with an enormous canopy might suggest a king's bedroom.

**Sentimental comedy** — Type of play that centers on good, kind, well-meaning, middle-class characters who have social and family problems that are easily and happily resolved.

**Sensation scene** — A novel and spectacular effect used in a theatrical production, especially in the melodramas of the nineteenth century.

**Set** — The scenery or surroundings in which a play takes place.

**Shutters** — Two painted flats that are moved together at the back of the stage.

**"Slice of life"** — A stage presentation in which a specific environment is reproduced without altering it. All human experience is depicted, usually the ugly, painful lives of the deprived lower classes. The term was coined by the naturalists, headed by Émile Zola at the end of the nineteenth century.

**Socialist realism** — The only type of theater permitted in Russia under the Communist Party from 1936 to the mid-1980s. It was characterized by dramas written and staged in the realistic style. Such plays had to convey political messages and glorify the Soviet government.

**Stalls** — Term used in late nineteenth century England that referred to the area in the auditorium between the stage and the few rows of benches at the back, which was filled with comfortable seats. They became the best and most expensive seats in the theater.

**Star system** — System that dominated the acting profession of the nineteenth century. Individual talented performers were featured in plays and the other performers were subordinate to the stars.

**Sturm und drang (or Storm and stress)** — A literary movement of the 1770s in Germany. Plays rebelled against established authority. Characters in these plays act according to instinct in a mysterious world that doesn't make sense. These plays range in subject, constantly change scene, and journey through time.

**Super-marionette** — Reference by English designer Edward Gordon Craig, indicating his desire for actors who can do anything the director asks, who will obediently do as the director orders.

**Surrealism** — Literally "beyond realism." Writers

in this movement worked spontaneously to get at deeper truths in the unconscious mind.

**Symbolism** — A style of theater in the late 1880s in France, which aimed to portray truth beyond what we see; to hint at and suggest through poetic language and symbols that convey concepts and feelings.

**Theater-in-the-round (or Arena stage)** — A circular stage that looks like a circus ring in which the audience is seated completely around the playing space.

**Theater of the absurd** — Refers to the work of playwrights, particularly of the 1950s, who felt the world was bleak, purposeless, and meaningless and wished to create theatrical images to convey this idea.

**Theater of Cruelty** — Term coined by Frenchman Antonin Artaud to label his idea of theater as an experience so powerful that it gets at the subconscious mind of each individual, makes spectators uncomfortable, and forces them to confront themselves.

**Thrust stage (or Open stage)** — Stage in which the audience is seated on three sides of a long, raised platform built against one wall of the auditorium.

**Tonnelet** — A round wicker frame with a short skirt attached to it that fell to the actor's knees on male costumes in eighteenth century France.

**Underground theater (also Minor or Illegitimate theater)** — In eighteenth century England these were theaters not licensed by the Lord Chamberlain. Entertainment there included puppet shows, concerts, pantomimes, and ballad operas.

**Verfremdungseffekt** — Literally "strange-making effect" or "distancing effect." Invented by German director Bertolt Brecht to remind the audience that what they are watching on stage reflects a problem or an attitude in the real world. The audience was interrupted from their emotional involvement with the characters by having situations made strange enough so the audience would ask questions, evaluate, and act on what they saw. Many devices were used to jar the audience from their involvement, from interspersing scenes with film and slides to showing the source of light on stage.

**Well-made play** — Carefully constructed play written by formula with complicated and carefully worked out stories with startling situations and intrigues to keep the plot moving. Refers to the plays of French playwrights Eugene Scribe and Victorien Sardou in the nineteenth century.

# SUGGESTED READING

Barranger, Milly S. *Theatre*. Belmont, CA: Wadsworth Publishing Co., 1986.

Brockett, Oscar G. *The Essential Theatre*, Fourth Edition. New York: Rinehart and Winston, Inc., 1988.

Cohen, Robert. *Theatre*, Second Edition. Mountain View, CA: Mayfield Publishing Co., 1988.

Hartnoll, Phyllis. *The Concise History of Theatre*. New York: N. Abrams, n.d.

Harwood, Ronald. *All the World's a Stage*. Boston: Little, Brown and Co., 1984.

Smiley, Sam. *Theatre: The Human Art*. New York: Harper & Row, 1987.

# INDEX

## A

Abbey Theatre, 63-4
Acting, romantic style, 41-3
Actor-managers, 51
Actors, in eighteenth century
    England, 21-2
*Age of Gold, The*, 114
*Akropolis*, 125
*Amadeus*, 119, 120, 121
    photos, 119, 120
*Amphitryon 38*, 88
"Angry Young Men," 107
Anne, 18
Antoine, André, 60, 61
*Apocalypsis cum figuris*, 124, 125
    photo, 124
Apollinaire, Guillaume, 82
Appia, Adolphe, 74, 75
    set designs, photos, 74
Arden, John, 107
*Arms and the Man*, 63
Artaud, Antonin, 92, 93-4
    photo, 93
Ashcroft, Peggy, 90
Astley, Philip, 45
Atlan, Lillian, 121
Audiences, rioting, 25
Augier, Emile, 48
Avant garde (France), 82-3

## B

*Baal*, 99
*Bald Soprano, The*, 101-2, 103, 105
    photo, 105
Balzac, Honoré de, 43
Bancroft, Squire, 51
    photo, 51,
*Barber of Seville, The*, 31
Baron, Michel, 32
Barrie, James M., 72-3
Bateman, Ellen, 46, 47
    illustration, 46
Bateman, Kate, 46, 47
    illustration, 46
Baylis, Lillian, 90

Beaumarchais, Pierre Augustin
    Caron de, 31-2
Beckett, Samuel, 101, 102, 103
    photo, 103
*Bedroom Farce*, 121
Beerbohm Tree, Herbert, 53
*Beggar's Opera, The*, 20, 23
    illustration, 23
Behan, Brendan, 108-9
Bellamy, Mrs., 27
Berman, Ed, 115
Bernhardt, Sarah, 32, 49-50
    photo, 32
Betty, William Henry West, 46, 47
    illustration, 46
*Birthday Party, The*, 121
*Blacks, The*, 104, 106
Blin, Roger, 94, 101
*Blind, The*, 71
*Blithe Spirit*, 88, 89
    photo, 89
*Blood Wedding*, 87
*Blue Bird, The*, 72
Bond, Edward, 107, 115
Boswell, James, 25
Boucicault, Dion, 48-9
    photo, 48
Brahm, Otto, 61-2
*Breasts of Tiresias, The*, 82
*Breath*, 102
Brecht, Bertolt, 92, 94-100
    German opposition to his plays, 99
    his actors, 98-9
    influence, 100
Brenton, Howard, 119
Breton, André, 81
Brook, Peter, 94, 116-7, 118-9
Büchner, Georg, 42
*Butchers, The*, 61

## C

Čapek, Karel, 79
*Caretaker, The*, 121, 122
    photo, 122
*Caste*, 52, 53
    photo, 52

*Caucasian Chalk Circle, The*, 97, 98,
    99
    photo, 97
*Cavalcade*, 88
*Chairs, The*, 104, 105
    photo, 105
Charles II, 18
Chausée, Pierre-Claude Nivelle de la,
    30
Chekhov, Anton, 64-5
*Cherry Orchard, The*, 65
    photos, 65
Children in early theater, 14-5
Children's theater, 130-1
    festivals, 130
    in England, 130-1
    in the Unified States, 130
*Chorus of Disapproval, A*, 120
Churchill, Caryl, 121, 123
Cibber, Colley, 19, 26, 27
Cibber, Suzannah, 21-2, 24
Clairon, Mademoiselle, 32, 34
Clive, Kitty, 23
Cloak-and-sword dramas, 14
*Cloud 9*, photo, 123
*Colleen Baun, The*, 48
Comédie Française, 32, 43
    photo, 43
Commedia dell'arte, 13-5, 30
*Conscious Lovers, The*, 19
*Constant Prince, The*, 125
Cooke, George Frederick, 42
Copeau, Jacques, 83-4, 92
Covent Garden Theatre, riot at,
    illustration, 24
Coward, Noel, 88, 92
Craig, Edward Gordon, 75-6
    set design, photo, 75
*Cyrano de Bergerac*, 72
    photo, 72

## D

Dadaism, 81
*Dame aux camélias, La*, 47, 48
    illustration, 47

Danchenko, Vladimir Nemirovich, 64, 66
Darwin, Charles, 60
Delaney, Shelagh, 108
*Deputy, The*, 112, 113
  photo, 112
Devine, George, 106, 107
Devrient, Ludwig, 41, 49
Diderot, Denis, 30
Director, 78
*Dog of Montargis, The*, 45
*Doll's House, A*, 58
  photo, 58
*Dream Play, A*, 73
  photo, 73
*Drums in the Night*, 95
Dumas, Alexandre, fils, 48
*Dumb Waiter, The*, 121
Dumesnil, Mademoiselle, 32, 34
Duse, Eleanora, 49

**E**

Edinburgh International Festival, 129
*Endgame*, 102, 103
  photo, 103
*Enemy of the People, An*, 58-9
English Restoration, 14, 15
English theater, 17-28, 62-3, 88-9, 109
  eighteenth century theater, 17-28
  entertaining theater, 88-9
  government support for, 109
Environmental theater, 113-4
Epic theater, 95-6
*Equus*, 121
Evans, Edith, 89, 90
  photo, 89
Expressionism, 79-81
  acting style, 81
  lighting, 80
  production style, 80

**F**

*Fantasticks, The*, 72
Fantasy plays, 72-3
*Father, The*, 59, 60
  photo, 59
*Faust*, 37
Fielding, Henry, 18
*First Distiller, The*, 85
Foote, Samuel, 20
*Formosa*, 45
Freie Bühne, 61-2

French Revolution, theater before, 32-3, 34-5
  actors and actresses, 32-3
    illustration, 33
  costumes and makeup, 34-5
Freud, Sigmund, 73
Fringe theater (England), 114, 115-6
*From Morn to Midnight*, 80

**G**

*Galileo*, 99
Galli-Bibiena, Giuseppe, design by, illustration, 29
Galli-Bibiena family, 29-30
García Lorca, Federico, 87-8, 92
Garrick, David, 21, 22-4, 25-6
  as actor-manager, 23
  illustration, 22
  influence on theater, 23-4
  staging changes, 25-6
*Gas*, 80
Gay, John, 20
Genet, Jean, 94, 104-5, 106
  actors and production style, 106
George II, 56
German documentary drama, 111, 113
German theater, 35-6, 61-2
  playwriting trends, 35-6
*Ghost Sonata, The*, 73
*Ghosts*, 58
Gielgud, John, 89, 90
  photo, 89
Gilbert, W.S., 53
Giraudoux, Jean, 87, 88, 92
Goethe, Johann Wolfgang von, 36-7, 38-9
Gogol, Nikolai, 47
Goldoni, Carlo, 30
Goldsmith, Oliver, 19-20
*Good Person of Setzuan, The*, photo, 97
*Good Woman of Sezuan, The*, 95, 98, 99
Gorbachev, Mikhail, 125
Gorky, Maxim, 60, 68-9
Gottsched, Johann, 35, 36
*Götz von Berlichingen*, 36
Gozzi, Carlo, 30
Grand Magic Circus, 114
Gray, Simon, 119
*Grecian Daughter, The*, 26
Gregory, Augusta, 63, 64
Grein, Jacob Thomas, 62, 63, 115

Grotowski, Jerzy, 94, 123, 125
  "holy actor," 123, 125
Guthrie, Tyrone, 90

**H**

*Hair*, 115
Hall, Peter, 116
*Happy Days*, 102
Hauptmann, Gerhart, 60, 62
Havel, Vaclav, 126-7
*Hay Fever*, 88
Hebbel, Friedrich, 47
*Hernani*, 42, 43
Hitler, Adolf, 99
*H.M.S. Pinafore*, 53
Hochhuth, Rolf, 111, 113, 115
*Home*, 53
*Homecoming, The*, 121
  photo, 121
Horniman, Annie, 63
*House of Bernarda Alba, The*, 87
*How the Other Half Loves*, 121
Hugo, Victor, 42
*Hurrah, We Live!*, 94

**I**

Ibsen, Henrik, 57-9
*Importance of Being Earnest, The*, 53
  photo, 53
*In the Shadow of the Glen*, 64
*Increased Difficulty of Concentration, The*, photo, 126
Independent theaters, 69
Independent Theatre Society, 62
*Inspector General, The*, 47
International Centre of Theatre Research, 118
*Intruder, The*, 72
*Investigation, The*, 111
Ionesco, Eugene, 101-2, 103-4
Irish theater, 63-4, 90-2
Irving, Henry, 55
Italian Renaissance theater, 13

**J**

Jarry, Alfred, 82-3
Jellicoe, Ann, 119
Jessner, Leopold, 81, 94
*Jet of Blood*, 94
Jones, Henry Arthur, 53
Jouvet, Louis, photo, 88
*Juno and the Paycock*, 92
  photo, 92
*Juristen*, 113

**K**

Kaiser, Georg, 79, 80
Kean, Charles, 53, 55
Kean, Edmund, 41-2, 49, 51
Kemble, John Philip, 26, 41
*King Ubu*, 82
   illustration, 82
Kortner, Fritz, 81
Kotzebue, August von, 43

**L**

*League of Youth, The*, 58
Lecouvreur, Adrienne, 32, 35
Lekain, Henri-Louis, 34
   illustration, 34
Lessing, Gotthold Ephraim, 35-6
Licensing Act of 1737, 18, 20, 115
Lighting, 25-6, 55, 75-6, 80
   changes made by David Garrick,
     25-6
   expressionist, 80
   in nineteenth century theater, 55
Lillo, George, 18-9
Littlewood, Joan, 107-8
   photo, 108
*London Merchant, The; or, the History
   of George Barnwell*, 18
*Look Back in Anger*, 106, 107
   photo, 107
*Loss of the Royal George, The*, 45
Louis XVI, 31
Loutherbourg, Philippe Jacques de,
   26
*Love's Last Shift; or, the Fool in
   Fashion*, 19
*Lower Depths, The*, 69
Lugné-Poë, Aurélian-François, 71
Lyubimov, Yuri, 125-6

**M**

Macklin, Charles, 21
Macready, William Charles, 50, 53
   photo, 50
*Madwoman of Chaillot, The*, 88
Maeterlinck, Maurice, 71-2
*Magnificent Cuckold, The*, 85
   setting for, illustration, 85
*Mahabharata, The*, 119
*Maid of Orleans, The*, 38
*Major Barbara*, 62, 63
   photo, 62
Makeup, in nineteenth century
   theater, 55
*Marat/Sade*, 111, 112, 117
   photo, 112

Marivaux, Pierre de, 30-1
   illustration of production, 31
Marlowe, Christopher, 14
*Marriage of Figaro, The*, 31
Martin, Mary, 73
Martin, Steve, 72
*Mary Stuart*, 37, 38
   photo, 37
*Masses and Man*, 80
Meiningen Players, 56
   photo, 56
Melodrama, 43-7
   dogs and children in, 45-7
   illustration, 44
*Memories, Dreams and Illusions*,
   photo, 132
Meyerhold, Vsevolod, 84-6
*Midsummer Night's Dream, A*, 54, 117
   photos, 54, 117
*Miss Julie*, 60
*Miss Sara Sampson*, 36
Mnouchkine, Ariane, 94, 113
Modjeska, Helena, 50
*Month in the Country, A*, 47
Moscow Art Theatre, 64
*Mother Courage and Her Children*, 95,
   97, 98, 99
   photo, 97
Moudoues, Rose Marie, 130
"Mudie, Miss," 47
Music halls, 47
*My Fair Lady*, 63

**N**

National Theatre (England), 116
Naturalism, 60
Neoclassical drama, 14
Neuber, Carolina, 35
   illustration, 35
Nicholas I, 47
Nicholas II, 47
Nichols, Peter, 119
Nineteenth century theater, 41-56
   actor-managers, 51
   actors and actresses, 50
   evolution of acting, 55-6
   in Europe, 47-9
   new theaters and playwrights in
     England, 52-3
   realism, 55
   Shakespeare rediscovered, 53-5
   "star system," 49-50
*Not I*, 102

**O**

O'Casey, Sean, 90, 92
*Octoroon, The*, 48
*Oedipus Rex*, photo, 77
*Old Heidelberg*, 61
Old Vic, 88, 90
Olivier, Lawrence, 89, 90, 116
   photo, 89
Osborne, John, 106-7, 115

**P**

*Pelléas and Mélisande*, 71
*Peter Pan*, 72-3
*Pillars of Society, The*, 58
Pinero, Arthur, 53
Pinter, Harold, 121
Pirandello, Luigi, 86-7, 92
Piscator, Erwin, 94
*Pisces*, 115
Pixérécourt, René Charles Guilbert
   de, 43-4, 45
Planchon, Roger, 114
*Playboy of the Western World, The*, 63,
   64
   photo, 63
*Plough and The Stars, The*, 90, 91, 92
   photos, 91
Poel, William, 76
Poor Theatre, 123
*Power of Darkness, The*, 68
Pritchard, Hannah, 26
*Private Lives*, 88
*Pygmalion*, 63

**Q**

*Quare Fellow, The*, 108
Quin, James, 21

**R**

Rachel (Éliza Félix), 49, 50
   photo, 50
*Rasputin*, 95
Realism, 57-61, 71-8
   acting techniques, 61
   production styles, 61
   revolts against, 71-8
   selective, see Selective realism
Reddish, Samuel, illustration, 19
Reinhardt, Max, 76-8, 94
Religious drama, 13
Renaud, Madeleine, 102
Rich, John, 20
Richardson, Ralph, 90
Rigby, Cathy, 73

Ristori, Adelaide, 50
*Rivals, The*, 20
*Robbers, The*, 37
    illustration, 37
Robertson, Tom, 52-3
*Robinson and Crusoe*, photo, 131
Roman theater, 13
*Romanesques, Les*, 72
Romantic drama, 42-3
    in France, 42-3
Romanticism, 72
*Room, The*, 121
Rostand, Edmond, 72
*Roxanne*, 72
Royal Academy of Dramatic Art, 53
*Royal Hunt of the Sun, The*, 121
Royal National Theatre, photo, 116
Royal Shakespeare Company, 116
*R.U.R.*, 79
    photo, 79
Russian theater, 64, 84-6
    biomechanics of acting, 85
    constructivist settings, 84-5
    experimental, 84-5
    state-controlled, 85-6

**S**

*Saint Joan*, photo, 62
Salvini, Tommaso, 50
Scene design, 26, 75-6
    changes made by David Garrick, 26
Schiller, Friedrich von, 36-7
*School for Scandal, The*, 20
    illustration, 20
Schröder, Friedrich Ludwig, 36
    illustration, 36
*Screens, The*, 104, 106
    photo, 106
Scribe, Eugene, 48
    "well-made plays," 48
*Seagull, The*, 64, 65, 66
    photo, 65
Selective realism, 72
*1789*, 113-4
*1793*, 113
*Shadow of a Gunman, The*, 90
Shaffer, Peter, 119
Shakespeare, William, 14, 53-4
    rediscovered in nineteenth century
        England, 53-4

Shakespearean England, theater in,
    14
Shaw, George Bernard, 63
*She Stoops to Conquer*, 19, 20
    photo, 19
Sheridan, Richard Brinsley, 19-20
Siddons, Sarah Kemble, 26, 27, 41
Siddons, William, 27
*Six Characters in Search of an Author*,
    86, 87
    photo, 87
*Society*, 53
*Soldiers, The*, 113, 115
Spain, Golden Age of, 14
Spectacle, 44-5, 76-8
Stalin, Josef, 86, 99
Stanislavsky, Konstantin, 64, 66,
    67-9
    *An Actor Prepares*, 68
    *My Life in Art*, 68
    new acting style, 68
    photo, 66
    production design, 67-8
Steele, Richard, 19
Stoppard, Tom, 119
Story, David, 107
*Streets of London, The*, 44-5
Strindberg, August, 59-60, 73, 92
    dream plays, 73
*Sturm und Drang*, 36-7
Surrealism, 81-2
Symbolism, 71-2
Synge, John Millington, 64

**T**

Talma, François-Joseph, 33, 34
    illustration, 33
Terry, Ellen, 54, 55
    photo, 54
Theater of Cruelty, 93-4
Theater of the Absurd, 101
Theatre Act of 1843, 52
Theatre Act of 1968, 115
*Theatre and Its Double, The*, 94
Théâtre du Soleil, 113
Théâtre Libre, 60
Theatre Royal Covent Garden,
    illustration, 17
*Thérèse Raquin*, 60
Thorndike, Sybil, 90

*Three Sisters, The*, 65, 67
    photo, 67
*Threepenny Opera, The*, 95, 96
    photo, 96
Toller, Ernst, 79, 94
Tolstoy, Alexei, 95
Tolstoy, Leo, 60, 68
*Transfiguration*, 79
Turgenev, Ivan, 47
*Tzar Fyodov Ivanovitch*, 67
Tzara, Tristan, 81

**U**

*Uncle Vanya*, 65
*Under the Gaslight*, 44
Underground theaters, 20

**V**

*Verfremdungseffekt*, 95
Vestris, François, 34, 51
    illustration, 34
Vieux Colombier, photo, 84
Voltaire (Francois-Marie Arouet), 30

**W**

*Waiting for Godot*, 101, 102
*Weavers, The*, 61, 62
    photo, 61
Weigel, Helene, 99
    photo, 99
Weiss, Peter, 111
Wesker, Arnold, 107
*Widower's House*, 63
Wilde, Oscar, 53
Wilks, Robert, 21
*William Tell*, 38
Wilton, Marie, 51
Woffington, Peg, 23, 24
Women playwrights, 121, 123
*Woodsman's Hut, The*, 44
World War II, effect on European
    theater, 100
*Woyzech*, 42

**Y**

Yeats, William Butler, 63
*Yerma*, 87

**Z**

Zola, Émile, 60